# THE FLIGHT OF
# RUDOLF
# Hess

## Other books by Roy Conyers Nesbit

*Woe to the Unwary*
*Torpedo Airmen*
*The Strike Wings*
*Target: Hitler's Oil* (with Ronald C. Cooke)
*Arctic Airmen* (with Ernest Schofield)
*Failed to Return*
*An Illustrated History of the RAF*
*RAF Records in the PRO* (with Simon Fowler, Peter
  Elliott and Christina Goulter)
*The Armed Rovers*
*The RAF in Camera 1903–1939*
*Eyes of the RAF*
*The RAF in Camera 1939–1945*
*The RAF in Camera 1945–1995*
*Coastal Command in Action 1939–1995*
*RAF: An Illustrated History from 1918*
*Britain's Rebel Air Force* (with Dudley Cowderoy and
  Andrew Thomas)
*RAF in Action 1939–1945*
*The Battle of Britain*
*The Battle of the Atlantic*

# THE FLIGHT OF
# RUDOLF
# Hess
## Myths and Reality

Roy Conyers Nesbit and Georges Van Acker

SUTTON PUBLISHING

This book was first published in 1999 by
Sutton Publishing Limited · Phoenix Mill
Thrupp · Stroud · Gloucestershire · GL5 2BU

This paperback edition first published in 2002

British Library Cataloguing in Publication Data
A catalogue record for this book is available from the
British Library

ISBN 0 7509 3185 X

Typeset in 11/13pt Imprint.
Typesetting and origination by
Sutton Publishing Limited.
Printed and bound in Great Britain by
J.H. Haynes & Co. Ltd, Sparkford.

# Contents

*For Wilma Van Acker
who endured with patience her husband's
preoccupation with Rudolf Hess for more
than seven years*

# Acknowledgements

The authors would like to acknowledge the assistance of Flight Officer Felicity Ashbee, WAAF; Hank Brown, NASM Smithsonian Institution, Archives Division, Washington D.C.; *Oberstleutnant a. D.* Bruno Carl; Frederick A. Dieter, NASM Smithsonian Institution, Archives Division, Washington D.C.; Jean Dillen; Dr Rolf Doberitz, *Deutscher Wetterdienst, Seewetteramt,* Hamburg; The Lord Selkirk of Douglas; Michael Fowler; Simon Fowler, Public Record Office; *Oberstabsfeldwebel* J. Fritsch, Bundeswehr IV.Korps, Potsdam Wildpark; Dr Fuchs, *Archivdirektor Bayerisches Hauptstaatsarchiv* München; Martin Garnett, Dept of Exhibits and Firearms, Imperial War Museum, London; His Grace the 15th Duke of Hamilton; Oliver Hoare, Public Record Office; G.L. Hope, Head of Tidal Branch, Hydrographic Office, MoD, Taunton; *Oberst a. D.,* Werner Horst; the late *Flugkapitän* Helmut Kaden; Siegfried Knoll; the late Wing Commander C. Hector Maclean; Lieutenant-Colonel John L. McCowen; Eric Mombeek; National Archives Records Service, Washington D.C.; Michael Oakey, *Aeroplane Monthly*; the late Flight Lieutenant Maurice A. Pocock RAFVR; Dr R. Reinke, *Deutscher Wetterdienst Zentralamt*, Offenbach; Winston G. Ramsey *After the Battle*; Karl Ries; Hanfried Schliephake; General Paul Sharp, NATO Brussels; the late Dr 'F.S.', former meteorologist; Paul Silberman, NASM Smithsonian Institution, Archives Division, Washington D.C.; Charles J. Thompson; M.J. Wood, Meteorological Office, Bracknell, Berkshire; Mrs Arline Youngman; Gerrit J. Zwanenburg.

To all of them our sincere thanks and gratitude for their highly valued help.

We also wish to thank the following owners of copyright, who gave us permission to quote from published works, or to reproduce photographs and documents from their collection: Mrs Heleen den Beer Poortugael, editor, for article in *Schipholland*, Amsterdam Airport; Mrs Jeanette Kalman for articles published in *Svenska Dagbladet*, Stockholm; Luc Van Loon for articles published in *Gazet Van Antwerpen*; Hans J. Ebert, Daimler-Benz Aerospace, Ottobrunn, for use of photographs; and Christiaan Vanhee, for use of photographs and rare German documents from his extensive collection.

Special thanks to Jean-Louis Roba for hitherto unknown details about Reinhard Heydrich's flying career, his information about the First World War and use of rare photographs. A special mention must also go to Wolf Rüdiger Hess, who answered numerous questions from us and lent us many photographs from his private collection. He also gave us permission to quote extensively from Ilse Hess's book *Ein Schicksal in Briefen* and we thank him for the invaluable help he has given us.

# Foreword

## BY THE DUKE OF HAMILTON

At dusk on 10 May 1941 Hess parachuted on to a Scottish moor just south of Glasgow and was taken into custody. He gave a false name and said he had an important message for my father, whom he said he had seen at the Berlin Olympics in 1936, although they had never met. Early next morning, my father, who was on duty at RAF Turnhouse, was told that a German pilot had crashed and was asking for him by name. He went to see the prisoner who identified himself as Hess and said that he wished to meet the king and other British leaders, to make a peace overture on behalf of Hitler. The main proposal was that, in return for allowing Germany freedom of action in Europe and Russia, Britain would get a free hand in most of her Empire. Later that day my father flew south to report to Churchill.

Hess's arrival aroused widespread speculation. Bizarre hypotheses abounded and within a year my father was obliged to bring a successful libel action against the general secretary of the British Communist Party. His death in 1973 diminished the inhibitions of the more fanciful theorists, since when there has been a marked increase in the number of imaginative theories published.

The authors of this book have drawn heavily on official documents in Germany, the USA and the Public Record Office at Kew. Early papers include a forty-page German report on Hess in the First World War, which gives precise details of his wounds and refers to his mental state. Later papers include those released in the 1990s by the Foreign Office, concerning the involvement of the SOE and MI5 in the affair. There is a detailed account of his preparations for the flight, as well as technical details of the aircraft modified for the purpose. There follows a vivid description of the flight, the efforts of the RAF to shoot him down and, not least, his difficulties in baling out of his aircraft. His life as a prisoner in British hands is covered, as is his trial at Nuremberg and long imprisonment at Spandau. Accounts of his various attempts at suicide are also given, including the final successful one at the age of 93. The book is annotated throughout with references and the narrative is accompanied by a series of remarkable photographs, some published for the first time.

The final chapter, 'Some of the Myths', tackles most of the outlandish interpretations of the Hess saga. Examples are those which claim that Hess was not the only person involved, that Hitler knew of or even authorized the flight, or that the man who arrived in Scotland was not Hess at all. There is also a frequently repeated contention that British military intelligence persuaded Hess to make his flight and another that my father was actively involved. Despite the authors' earnest efforts to deal with at least the wilder theories, it seems inevitable that more will emerge and that the 'Hess Conspiracy' industry will remain in business for some time.

It is not easy to be scholarly and entertaining. Nesbit and Van Acker have managed to be both and wear their scholarship lightly. Their research has been exhaustive and their judgement is shrewd. They present technical details simply. Above all, they can tell a story. Theirs is a truth which may be stranger than fiction, but it is clear, concise and entertaining.

# Introduction

The western world appears to be more interested in Rudolf Hess than in any other Nazi leader, with the exception of Adolf Hitler. His astonishing flight from Augsburg to Scotland on 10 May 1941, in an attempt to negotiate peace between Britain and Germany, has given rise to much curiosity and speculation. His long and mostly solitary incarceration in Spandau Prison, before his death on 17 August 1987 at the age of 93, has weighed heavily on the consciences of many observers and commentators.

Many books and articles have been written about Hess, describing his life in some detail from early childhood to death. In all these the main subject remains his daring and skilled flight. Some authors even go so far as to describe in detail every move that Hess made and his thoughts during this flight, as though they were looking over his shoulder at the time and were also able to read his mind. However, there are wide variations in these accounts, for they make different assumptions and then advance different theories.

Among the theories put forward by these authors can be found the following: there were two pilots and two aircraft involved; Hess made an intermediate landing at Schiphol airport; he took off from Calais airfield; he was lured to Britain by British military intelligence; the RAF anticipated his flight and allowed the aircraft to pass unhindered across Northumberland and Scotland; one of the drop-tanks from his aircraft was found in the Clyde; the pilot was not Hess but an imposter flying to Scotland for some unexplained reason; he did not commit suicide in Spandau prison but was murdered.

Most of these authors also try to prove their assumptions by using selective evidence, ignoring or dismissing facts which are readily available in British and German public records. The results are known as 'conspiracy theories' and we must advise the reader that none will be advanced in this book, although some will be examined and criticized.

The purpose of this book is to provide a straightforward account of Hess's life and his flight to Scotland, using reliable sources of reference such as the Public Record Office in Kew, the Bayerisches Hauptstaatarchiv in Munich, Daimler-Benz Aerospace in Ottobrun, the National Archives and Records Administration in Washington DC, the Archives Division of the Smithsonian Institution in Washington DC, various other official sources and the accounts of several eye-witnesses to the events. We do not intend to advance further theories about Hess's motives for his flight, although we have discovered a few additional facts which may prove useful to other researchers; in our opinion by far the most reliable account of his motives is presented in *The Truth About Rudolf Hess* by James Douglas-Hamilton, published in 1993 after the release of numerous documents relating to Hess by the Public Record Office.

We have concentrated on certain episodes in Hess's life, such as those which show his ability as a pilot and his preparation for the flight, in order to demonstrate the inaccuracy of some of the conspiracy theories. We hope that our account, suitably annotated with references, will resolve many of the riddles which still bedevil this strange episode of the Second World War.

Roy Conyers Nesbit, Wiltshire, England, 2002
Georges Van Acker, Kontich, Belgium, 2002

# CHAPTER ONE

# Student, Soldier and Aviator

For several months in early 1941 Hess had been poring over maps of north-west Europe, the boundaries of the North Sea, the northern sector of Northumberland and the south of Scotland. He had been living in a world of aircraft instruments and piston pressures, cooling water temperatures and oxygen supplies, aircraft performance figures and synoptic charts – not to mention all the other details studied by aircrew preparatory to a long-distance flight. Now he was on his way at last, convinced that the most important mission of his life would succeed.

The German weather forecast was favourable, indicating a large anti-cyclone to the west of Britain, with light westerly winds over Germany and the Low Countries veering northerly over the North Sea. Cloud was scattered and visibility was good. Unknown to Hess, the British forecast indicated light variable winds over north-east England and south-west Scotland, where conditions were expected to be mainly cloudy with a few showers. Hess had chosen an excellent day.

Hess was justifiably proud of his skill in making the historic solo flight from Bavaria to Scotland. Some weeks later while in captivity, he wrote a long letter home to his son 'Buz', knowing that its contents would be read aloud to the boy by his wife Ilse, who might also pass the information on to those competent enough to understand his methods and admire his achievement. But even if Ilse kept the information to herself for the time being, Hess was recording his daring flight for posterity.

Rudolf Hess was kept incarcerated for another forty-six years, a hapless pawn in the relentless Cold War game of chess between East and West until, in 1987, he took his own life in Berlin's Spandau prison. His body was eventually laid to rest in the family plot at Wunsiedel where the simple headstone bears the inscription 'Ich Hab's Gewagt', which translated means 'I dared'.

Rudolf Walter Richard Hess was born on 26 April 1894 in Ibrahimieh, an eastern suburb of Alexandria in Egypt. The villa was not far from Aboukir, the scene of Nelson's victory over the French fleet on 1 August 1798 which established the Royal Navy's domination of the Mediterranean. Rudolf's father was Fritz Hess, a wealthy merchant who owned the trading firm of Hess & Co. This company had been established by Rudolf's grandfather Christian Hess, who married Margarete Bühler and emigrated to Egypt in 1865 together with their son and two daughters.[1] The Hess family originated from Wunsiedel, about 95 km north-west of Nuremberg, in the Fichtelgebirge. Fritz also owned a house in Reicholdsgrün, about 10 km north-west of Wunsiedel. His wife was Klara Münch, the daughter of a textile manufacturer. Rudolf was the eldest of their three children, his brother Alfred being born in 1897 and his sister Margarete in 1908.[2]

The family lived in a large and beautiful three-storey villa, surrounded by a magnificent garden. The desert stretched eastwards from the garden wall, while to the west was the fairy-tale city of Alexandria with its port, splendid buildings and bazaars. To the north, a golden beach fringed the turquoise waters of the Mediterranean. Life for the family was very comfortable and even idyllic in some respects. The parents gave parties from time to time, their guests usually being members of the German colony in Alexandria, but for the most part their private life was centred on their children.[3]

The two boys attended the German Protestant School in Alexandria, Rudolf from 1900 to 1906. From 1900 the family travelled to Germany every year during the summer, where they spent several weeks in their house in Reicholdsgrün. After initial schooling, the two brothers received private tuition from an Egyptian tutor, Abdul Aziz *Effendi* (Master), but they never learnt to speak Arabic. Much to the disappointment of their father, neither boy showed any interest in the family firm or any desire to take over its management. Rudolf was sent to Germany in 1908 and from 15 September of that year attended the Evangelical School in Bad Godesberg. Although his father still expected him to take over the family firm, he showed more interest in mathematics and science. This did not deter his father from sending him in 1911 to the Ecole Supérieur de Commerce at Neuchâtel in Switzerland. Rudolf left that school after a year and began an apprenticeship with a business firm in Hamburg.

By 1914 the population of the German Reich numbered 68 million, about 60 per cent more than when it was founded on 9 December 1870. Unemployment was low, there was little social need, and industries were thriving. Germany was becoming a very wealthy nation and in military terms was the most powerful in the world, with a large and well-equipped army as well as a modern navy which was regarded anxiously by both Britain and France, especially since Germany was casting covetous eyes on their overseas empires. The Triple Alliance of Germany, Austria-Hungary and Italy was confronted by the Triple Entente of Britain, France and Russia. Signs of an impending war were becoming more visible each day.

The event which sparked off the immense conflict was the assassination of the Archduke Franz Ferdinand of Habsburg-Este, heir to the throne of Austria-Hungary, and his consort Sophie Chotek, the duchess of Hohenburg, in Sarajevo in the morning of 28 June 1914.

The man who fired the revolver shots was Gavrilo Princip, a twenty-year-old member of a Serbian secret society known as the Black Hand which opposed the projected incorporation of Serbia into the Austro-Hungarian Empire.[4] On 28 July Austria-Hungary declared war on Serbia. Russia, which regarded Serbia as an ally, began to mobilize. Germany declared war on Russia on 1 August, and entered Luxembourg the following day to seize the railways needed for the passage of troops for an invasion of neutral Belgium. On 3 August Germany declared war on France and Britain declared war on Germany the following day. On 6 August Austria-Hungary was at war with Russia. The First World War had begun. Italy remained neutral at first but decided to come in on the side of the Triple Entente on 23 May 1915.

In August 1914 all the members of the Hess family were in their summer residence in Reicholdsgrün except the twenty-year-old Rudolf, who was still serving his apprenticeship in Hamburg. He left this position a few days later and joined his family. Against his father's wishes, he then travelled to Munich to join the ranks as a volunteer and on 20 August 1914 enlisted in the 7th Bavarian Field Artillery Regiment. After some initial training *Infanterist* (Private) Rudolf Hess was posted on 18 September to the 3rd Supplementary Company, 1st Supplementary Battalion, 1st Infantry Regiment.[5] This was stationed on the Western Front, opposite the British Expeditionary Force on the Somme.

Towards the end of October 1914 the Belgians had succeeded in inundating large areas on both sides of the River Ijzer (Yser), between Nieuwpoort and Bikschote. These defensive measures caused the Germans to withdraw from the region and the fighting came to a temporary halt. The Germans attacked again on 30 October, on a narrower front from the Messines Ridge to Gheluvelt, 5 miles east of Ieper (Ypres). It was here that

Rudolf Hess received his baptism of fire against the seasoned soldiers of the British I Corps.

The German forces included numerous recruits who were the flower of the country's youth, mostly students burning with zeal and patriotism. Waves after waves of these young men were thrown against British regular soldiers, who were trained in rapid fire with their bolt-action rifles. The young volunteers could be heard singing patriotic songs amid the din of fire from rifles, machine-guns and field guns, but they were mown down in their thousands. Nevertheless the Germans broke through at Gheluvelt and were only driven out by a fierce counter-attack from mixed battalions. They broke through again in places and the confused fighting continued for several days, with the outcome remaining in the balance until the attackers withdrew from exhaustion and enormous losses. The British lost about 50,000 men killed, wounded or missing in the battle, including a large part of their regular army. To their south the French lost a similar number. The German losses have never been released but must have been far greater. They described the battle as *Der Kindermord von Ypern*, which may be translated as 'The Massacre of the Innocents at Ypres'.

Rudolf Hess survived this slaughter, although the experience must have left a deep and lasting impression on him. Another participant was Adolf Hitler, who had enlisted as a volunteer in the 16th Bavarian Infantry Regiment, although the two men did not meet at this stage. Hitler's unit also suffered very severe casualties, and the future German Chancellor was recommended for the Iron Cross, Second Class, which was awarded to him on 2 November 1914, in the course of the fighting. The First Battle of Ypres ended the period of open warfare and the two sides dug into entrenched positions until the Germans made their final and unsuccessful push in 1918.

On 9 November 1914 Hess was transferred to the 1st

Company of the 1st Infantry Regiment, which was stationed near Arras in the Artois province of France.[6] He was promoted to *Gefreiter* (Corporal) on 21 April 1915 and six days later was awarded the Iron Cross, Second Class, for his bravery in the field. For six weeks from the end of August 1915 Hess underwent courses at the Army Training School at Munsterlager, where he attained the rank of *Vizefeldwebel* (Lance-Sergeant). On 22 October he received the M.V.K. (*Militärisches Verdienst Kreuz*, or Military Merit Cross) awarded by the Kingdom of Bavaria. Newly promoted and additionally decorated, he returned to his unit in the front line on 20 November, where he saw more action in the Artois sector. In early 1916 he participated in the battles for Neuville St Vaast, which was completely destroyed. Then a throat infection took him behind the lines on 20 February 1916 for more than two months. On 1 May he returned to his unit once more and took part in the gruesome Battle of Verdun.

The Germans had launched their offensive against the French lines in this sector on 21 February 1916. Their attacks had been successful at first, particularly in the area east of the River Maas, but the French resistance stiffened gradually and the battle became one of attrition, with terrible casualties on both sides. Towards the end of the month, the Germans captured the fort of Douaumont, which resembled a giant ruin when seen from the air. Nevertheless by April General Von Falkenhayn admitted that the German assault on Verdun was becoming a failure. In spite of this admission, he continued a series of pointless attacks.

On 12 June, while near Thiaumont village in the vicinity of Douaumont, Hess was wounded in the left hand and upper arm by splinters from an exploding shell, and sent to the *Reserve Lazarett* (reserve hospital) at Bad Homburg. He was transferred to the *Reserve Lazarett* at Ilsenburg on 28 June and remained there until 13 July, when he returned to his unit once more.[7] Von Falkenhayn called off his offensive in mid July, by which time the losses of all ranks amounted to 362,000 German and 336,800 French.

On 25 December 1916 Hess was posted to the 18th Bavarian Reserve Infantry Regiment and was appointed a platoon leader of the 10th Company. This unit was stationed in Romania, which had declared war on the Central Powers on 27 August 1916 in the hope of territorial gain in Transylvania. The move proved unwise, for her poorly officered troops were held in check while a force of Germans, Bulgarians and Turks attacked from the south, gaining control of much of the country including the capital, Bucharest. Hess took part in the Battle of Rimnicu Sârat, a town some 120 km north-north-east of Bucharest. On 23 July 1917, while at the Oituz Pass, he was hit once more in the left arm by another shell splinter.[8] On this occasion the wound was not considered serious enough to require hospital treatment. He remained with his unit, receiving treatment at a field dressing station. However, another wound he received on 8 August 1917 was far more serious and even life-threatening. At the storming of the Ungüreana, a small hill in the Carpathians near Focsani, 150 km north-north-east of Bucharest, he was shot through the body by a Romanian soldier.[9]

Hess arrived the following day at *Kriegslazarett* (Military Hospital) 21C at Bezdivasarhely in Hungary. On 11 August this hospital recorded that the bullet had entered the front of his chest near the left armpit, leaving a 'pea-sized' hole surrounded by puckered skin. It had passed through the lung and exited near the spinal column by the 4th vertebra, below the shoulder blade, leaving a 'cherry stone-sized' hole. The patient was spitting blood and there was some respiratory noise, but the wounds looked clean.

It is evident that Hess had been shot by a small calibre

rifle bullet, probably while advancing in a crouched attitude. Luckily for him the bullet had passed through his body without piercing the heart or striking any bones. On 20 August the hospital recorded that the spitting of blood had ceased and that on the whole the situation looked good. Four days later his fever had subsided, he was almost free of sweating and had regained his strength. It was considered that he should go back to the Fatherland, but on 26 August he was taken to *Kriegslazarett* 21B at Sepsiszentgyörgy, also in Hungary, for further medical treatment. He continued to make progress, with no coughing, no excess saliva and no problems with his heart, but with rather shallow breathing. This hospital also confirmed that, since his convalescence would last more than six weeks, he should be sent back to the Fatherland.

On 11 September Hess began his journey to Germany in Hospital Train no. 9. From 17 September to 23 October he was a patient at the *Reserve Lazarett* Meissen, 20 km west-north-west of Dresden. During this period, on 8 October, he was commissioned as a *Leutnant der Reserve*, officially confirmed a fortnight later. He was also recommended for the Iron Cross, First Class, although he never received this decoration. His father Fritz Hess had written to Meissen on 30 September asking for his son to be transferred to the hospital at Alexandersbad, since it was nearer the family home at Reicholdsgrün. This request was granted and on 25 October Hess arrived at the *Reserve Lazarett* Alexandersbad, 48 km north of Bayreuth, where he was again medically examined while recuperating from his wound. He was found to be in generally good health, with a regular pulse and improved breathing, but he frequently complained about his health and was considered to have a tendency towards hypochrondria.

The medical officers decided that he could be discharged from hospital as a *Kriegsverwendungsfähige* (fit for active service) in the 1st Supplementary Infantry Leib Regiment, Munich. However, during his convalescence, on 29 November, he put in a formal application for transfer from this unit:

I request to be posted to pilot training after the end of my cure, which terminates on 15 December 1917. I should have been posted to the Air Service in August of this year if I had not been wounded at this time. According to my doctor, my wound has healed to the point where I am fit again for flying duties. According to the enclosed testimony from my Company Commander, my nerves are equal to all demands. Also my eyes are first class. With regard to my initial training, I am familiar with the engines of motor bicycles and motor cars. So far as possible, I have prepared myself by reading technical books about flying.[10]

We do not know Hess's motives for pursuing this application for a transfer to the Air Service, but it is possible to make some informed guesses. He had spent three years in the infantry, much of this time in the front line, and had endured squalor, stench, poor food and constant shelling, while many of his comrades had been killed and he had been wounded three times. The expectation of life in the Air Service was even shorter, with heavy losses in combat and flying accidents, but there were some compensations. The men lived behind the lines in reasonably comfortable conditions and with better messing facilities. Military aviation was only a few years old, but its circumstances were fascinating, with the rapid advance of technology and the thrill of flying. All pilots were esteemed by the general public and fighter aces became popular heroes. There was still an element of chivalry in their operations. Although the general practice was to manoeuvre so as to shoot an opponent in the back, the pilots retained much respect for their enemies. It was even a common practice to drop messages on enemy airfields, giving news about those shot down behind their lines and asking for information of their own missing pilots.

Hess was granted convalescent leave on 11 December, which he spent at the family home in Reicholdsgrün until the last day of 1917. There was a strange coincidence in his life in January 1918, according to the woman he later married. While presumably on light duties following his return from convalescent leave, he was ordered to escort the List Regiment to the Western Front, where he reported to *Oberstleutnant* Anton, Freiherr von Tuboeuf. He noticed a *Gefreiter* standing near this officer. Although the two men did not speak to each other and Hess did not know the name of the corporal, he realized several years later that the man was Adolf Hitler.[11]

Meanwhile, on 6 April 1917 the USA had declared war on Germany, although American contingents did not reach the front line in France in any strength for over a year. Another event that was to have a major effect on the war was the Bolshevik Revolution in Russia in October 1917, which led to the Russo-German Armistice of 15 December and ultimately to a peace treaty that was ratified on 29 March 1918. Without her ally, Romania had to make peace with the Central Powers ten days later.

In January 1918 Hess went to Munich, where he passed the aptitude and medical tests for the Air Service, and on the 22nd of that month began a fortnight's leave at home. On 15 March he began a three-month course which commenced with ground instruction at *Fliegerschule 1* (Flying School 1) at Schleissheim, 12 km north of the centre of Munich. Such instruction normally included the theory of flight, the internal combustion engine, air navigation, aircraft armament, bombing procedures and meteorology. After a couple of months he began his *ab initio* flying training at *Fliegerschule 4*, based at *Lager* (Camp) Lechfeld, south of Augsburg. The type of elementary trainer he flew remains uncertain, but we know that it was a two-seater and that he crashed on his first solo cross-country flight, in a meadow near Ried am Ammersee, 35 km west-south-west of Munich. Much later, while in Spandau prison, he wrote a letter dated 20 September 1953 to his son Wolf Rüdiger which included the following: 'Luckily such a trainer had the pilot's seat at the back. If I had been sitting in the front seat it would have ended my career for this was rammed into the ground on impact.' The aircraft was a total loss but Hess escaped without injury.[12]

After completion of this initial training, somewhat delayed as a result of his crash, Hess was posted on 1 October to a *Luftpark* (Aircraft Transit Camp) and then to more advanced training at *Jagdstaffelschule 1* (Fighter Squadron School 1) at Valenciennes in France. By this time Germany's massive offensive on the Western Front, which began on 21 March 1918 with armies reinforced by troops released from the Eastern Front, had been repelled by the British and French with the strong aid of the Americans. The Germans were in full retreat everywhere and Allied aircraft dominated the skies.

On 14 October 1918 Hess joined a Bavarian fighter squadron, *Jagdstaffel 35b*.[13] This was based at Givry, north-east of Mons in Belgium, but on 29 October it moved to Gosselies, to the east of Charleroi. It was equipped with the Fokker D.VII, an aircraft which had begun to enter service in April 1918 and is generally accepted as Germany's finest fighter of the war. Photographs exist showing Hess in the cockpit of one of these machines. Another photo shows him wearing the collar insignia of a lieutenant and posing in front of a Fokker Dr.1 triplane.

However, the newly qualified pilot had arrived too late

to put his skills in combat to the test, for the war was reaching its inevitable end. In the last four months the Germans had lost 80,000 killed, 350,000 missing in action and 360,000 wounded. Even by the horrific standards of this war, such losses could not be sustained. The German military machine was broken, while at home civilians were nearing starvation from the effects of the Allied sea blockade. Negotiations between Allied and German delegates began on 8 November. An Armistice Treaty was signed and at 11.00 hours on 11 November 1918 the First World War finally came to an end.

# CHAPTER TWO

## *Politician and Aviator*

Hess's fighter squadron was disbanded after the war, as were most of the others in the German Air Force. The units were ordered by the Allies to transfer their aircraft and equipment to designated assembly points. Some of the aircraft were cannibalized but most of them were left in the open to rot away.

On 27 November 1918 Hess went on leave to Reicholdsgrün, and his military career came to an end when he was discharged from the armed forces on 13 December 1918. It can be imagined that he was thoroughly depressed and troubled. The British had appropriated the family company in Alexandria, leaving his parents with severe problems. He was twenty-four years of age, without formal qualifications and with little experience of earning a living in civilian life. It was difficult for him to digest the terms of the Armistice Treaty. Long years of warfare, with continual carnage and the loss of many comrades, leave an indelible mark on any man. Memories of such a conflict remain in the consciousness for the rest of one's life. Bitterness is lessened for the victors, but the defeated feel a deep sense of frustration and seek to find objects for their resentment. As a returned soldier and pilot, Hess had been moulded by warfare and fighting. In February 1919 he joined the Thule Society, which had been founded by *Freiherr* (Baron) Rudolf von Sebottendorff the previous year. This was a collection of fervent nationalist and anti-Semitic parties which were intent on overthrowing the *Räterepublik* – the Soviet Republic of Bavaria – which had been set up in that German state by the *Spartakusbund* (Spartacus League), a militant Communist organization engaged on attempts to take over the whole of Germany.

During violent skirmishes between the *Spartakists* and members of the Thule Society seven of the latter were captured, together with an innocent bystander, the Jewish Professor Berger, and taken hostage. On 30 April 1919 these eight hostages were summarily executed. As a result various troops entered Munich at the beginning of May to liberate the city from the grip of these 'Red Guards'. During fierce street battles on 1 May Hess was wounded yet again, this time in the leg. On 7 May he joined the *Freikorps*, led by General Franz Xaver Ritter von Epp, and continued in this unit against the *Spartakists* until resigning his commission at the end of April 1920.

Hess also decided to resume his education, as a student at Munich University. Acceptance was straightforward since former soldiers were exempt from entrance examinations. Although he did not aim at taking his *Abitur* (final degree examinations), he read economics and history and came under the influence of Major-General Professor Karl Haushofer, the exponent of Geopolitics, who propounded the idea of Germany's territorial expansion.[1] He had already met Haushofer, for in the summer of 1919 one of his friends had taken him to dinner at the professor's house. He became a close friend of the professor as well as one of his sons, Albrecht, who was to become a university lecturer and a highly respected exponent of social theories.

In April 1920 Ilse Pröhl, the daughter of *Oberstabsarzt* (Surgeon-Major) Dr Friedrich Pröhl, arrived in Munich by train from Berlin. After the death of her father, her mother and stepfather Carl Horn came to live near Lake Ammer, close to Munich. She was to take her *Abitur* at the university and had arranged to stay at a small boarding-house run by Fraulein von Schildberg in Schwabing, the students' quarter of Munich. Her room was not ready on her arrival and she sat for a while on a small landing, feeling a little tired after the long journey. She was slightly startled when a young man entered the house and began to leap up the stairs three at a time. He wore a field-grey uniform with the bronze lion of the *Freikorps Epp* on the left arm.[2] On noticing the young woman he stopped suddenly, clicked his heels and bowed, and then continued leaping up the stairs. Ilse saw that he was quite tall (in fact 1.77 metres, about 5 ft 10 in), well built, and had a square-cut face, deep-set eyes and bushy eyebrows.

It turned out that Rudolf and Ilse occupied adjacent rooms but at first the young man remained aloof, for he was rather reserved and preferred not to mix with the other guests. However, one day he approached her in a state of excitement and asked her to accompany him in two days' time to a beer tavern named *Sterneckerbräu* where, in a smoke-filled room, he had been listening to a speech by a man whose name he could not remember. Ilse liked the appearance and manner of this personable young man and accepted the invitation.[3] It transpired that the meeting was held by the *Deutsche Arbeiter Partei* (German Workers' Party, or DAP) and the speaker was a certain Adolf Hitler. To Hess, everything this man said was logical, clear, and unassailably correct, although Ilse remained somewhat sceptical.

Of course by this time Hitler had also left the army, having somehow survived four years of fighting in the front line, in the course of which he had been awarded the Iron Cross, First Class. Although his adult life before August 1914 had been shiftless and indolent, war service had exhilarated and moulded him. This mood had changed to one of black despair at the Armistice, when he was in hospital recovering from temporary blindness caused by a British gas attack. He emerged from the psychological shock with the irrational beliefs that

Germany's defeat was the fault of Jews and Bolsheviks and that he was the new Siegfried who would lead his country to vengeance on these enemies.

Normally nondescript and socially awkward, Hitler had the ability to deliver his views from the political platform with blazing force and powerful phrases. Nowadays, his speeches read as little more than hysterical ravings but there can be no doubt that at the time they drew on a wide and deep stream of opinion among audiences which consisted mainly of ex-servicemen burning with resentment at defeat and the reparations that Germany was expected to pay under the Treaty of Versailles which was being negotiated with the victorious Allies. These included the loss of territory to France, Poland and Belgium, partition of the African colonies, abolition of the High Seas Fleet and all warplanes, restriction of the army to 100,000 men, and the payment of immense amounts of gold and material wealth to the victors. Meanwhile, the Allies continued their blockade, to persuade Germany to accept the terms. Hitler, Hess and the majority of the audiences were *Frontschweine*, survivors of the 'poor bloody infantry' who had borne the brunt of the fighting and now formed a brotherhood of the trenches. These men felt that the sacrifices they and their comrades had made had been in vain and that they had been betrayed. Their country, so proud and confident before the war, had become impoverished and torn with ideological conflicts.

Certainly Hess was mesmerized by Hitler and in June 1920, a year after the Treaty of Versailles, he joined the *Nationalsozialistische Deutsche Arbeiterpartei* (National Socialist German Workers' Party or NSDAP) as the DAP had become. After this, he spent an increasing amount of time with Hitler and became his most faithful acolyte. As the movement gained popularity, the meetings of the NSDAP were held in the Hofbräuhaus in Munich, which could hold a larger audience. Hess was a hesitant and ineffective orator on the political platform. He concentrated instead on collecting funds for the Party and talking to students, when he was at his best while extolling the achievements of German heroes. After Hitler gave a speech to the students, Hess formed a Nazi group at Munich University in February 1921. He was injured again when, on 4 November 1921, he was struck violently on the head while protecting Hitler during an attempt by Marxists to blow up the Hofbräuhaus. It was on this occasion that Hitler gave his group of Nazi thugs its name, *Sturmabteilung* (Stormtroopers or SA), later known as 'Brown-shirts'.

By 1922 Hess himself had joined the SA, which was spreading all over Germany while the popularity of the Nazis was growing. The eleventh Nazi *Student-Hundertschaft* (Student-Hundred) was founded by Hess in November of that year.[4] The strength of the SA increased to 2,000 members by the end of the year but Hitler was beginning to lose control of this organization, which was becoming more of a militia group than a political protection force.

On 11 January 1923 French and Belgian troops occupied the Ruhr, on the pretext that Germany had failed to meet its obligations with respect to the reparations. The loss of the industrial heartland was a great blow to the German economy, fuelling hyper-inflation and creating massive unemployment. Hitler's cause benefited from the unrest which followed. The first Party Day of the Nazis was held in Munich on 28 January, although it had been prohibited by the Bavarian Chief of Police. The SA held a parade the following day, also in defiance of an official ban. Four months later there was unrest when the French arrested Albert Leo Schlageter, a member of the *Freikorps*. He was charged with espionage and sabotage of the railway near

Duisburg, and was executed on 26 May 1923 on Golzheimer Heath near Dusseldorf; eventually he was elevated to the status of a national hero.[5]

Towards the end of 1923 the Deutschmark had become worthless and the economy was in tatters. Hitler, believing his hour had come, attempted a *coup d'état* in Munich (the *Putsch*), in the hope that this would lead to control in Berlin. On 8 November he and his followers in the SA surrounded a meeting of local dignitaries in the *Bürgerbräukeller*. These included the State Commissioner, the Commander of the armed forces and the Chief of the Bavarian State Police, with about 3,000 people in the audience who were busy drinking ale from earthenware mugs. Suddenly Hitler burst in, together with Hess and the SA stormtroopers. He jumped on a chair, fired a revolver shot into the ceiling, and announced that a national revolution had begun.[6] He then invited the audience to join him in the new government that he was forming with the renowned General Erich Ludendorff, and appeared to gain the support of officials, including the State Commissioner. Meanwhile Hess and some stormtroopers rounded up some of the notables as 'enemies of the people' and took them by car to a house near Lake Tegern, about 50 km south-south-east of Munich.

The next day brought disaster for the Nazis. A march by several thousand people through the streets of Munich was met with gunfire from the Bavarian State Police and sixteen men were killed; the rest scattered. Meanwhile Hess's exploits ended in farce, for when he went outside to make a telephone call, his hostages persuaded the driver to take them back to Munich, leaving him stranded.[7] He managed to contact Ilse Pröhl, who brought assistance in the form of a bicycle, and he took refuge with the Haushofers.[8] Hitler was arrested at a friend's house the following day and taken to Landsberg am Lech prison, about 50 km south-south-west of Munich. Both the SA and the NSDAP had been outlawed.

Hitler's trial was held in Munich on 24 February 1924 and he was sentenced on 1 April to five years' imprisonment, but with the recommendation of an early release after six months. Hess had fled to Austria, where he went into hiding, but he gave himself up on the advice of Karl Haushofer and was sentenced to 18 months' imprisonment, with the promise of an early release. He joined Hitler and several others in the Landsberg prison. It was here that the majority of the work on *Mein Kampf* took place, with Hitler dictating to Hess, who edited the pages of the manuscript and checked them for errors, no doubt contributing some remarks of his own.

Hitler was released on 20 December 1924 and concentrated on building up his organization. Hess was released ten days afterwards and resumed his friendship with Karl Haushofer. On 26 February 1925 Hitler announced that the SA was to be re-founded and on the following day declared to a jubilant audience in the Bürgerbräukeller in Munich that the NSDAP was also to be re-founded. On the same day, Hess was appointed as his private secretary.

*Mein Kampf* was published in two parts, the first in July 1925 and the second in December 1926. Several years later the two parts were issued as a single book and eventually sold about 1½ million copies, principally after the Nazis came to power. Hitler had the benefit of royalties from this evil book while other financial support came from party members, industrialists and bankers. Hess accompanied his leader on many tours of Germany, becoming his closest confidant and preparing leaflets and posters.[9] At this time, Hitler created the *Schutzstaffel* (Protection Squad or SS), whose black-shirted members swore a personal oath of loyalty to him as his bodyguard.

These were the years when Hess was able to resume his

passion for aviation. On 20 and 21 May 1927 the American aviator Charles Lindberg made the first solo crossing of the Atlantic, flying non-stop in a single-engined Ryan NYP from Roosevelt Field in Long Island to Le Bourget near Paris and landing after a flight lasting thirty-three hours. At the time such feats were received with wild acclamation and Hess longed to cap the exploit by flying solo in the other direction, against the prevailing winds. He made extensive preparations for almost a year, seeking sponsorship from major industrial firms, but in the end his personal plans were defeated by financial difficulties.[10] The first non-stop crossing did eventually take place, on 12 and 13 April 1928, when Junkers W33L *Bremen*, serial D-1167, was flown from Baldonnel in Ireland and force-landed on Greenly Island, Labrador. It was crewed by Ehrenfried *Freiherr* von Hünefeld, Hermann W. Köhl and the Irishman James C. Fitzmaurice, thus improving Germany's international prestige.[11]

Hess's marriage to Ilse Pröhl took place on 20 December 1927, it is said on the advice of Hitler, who acted as a witness, together with Karl Haushofer; their son Wolf Rüdiger Adolf Karl was born much later, on 18 November 1937. During the summer of 1928 Hess spent some time with Hitler at the latter's rented villa.[12] Although his political involvement took up much of his time, his enthusiasm for flying still continued. On 4 April 1929 he gained his private pilot's licence at the *Fliegerschule* (Flying School) Fürth near Nuremberg. His flying instructor was Theo Croneiss, who later became a close collaborator of Willy Messerschmitt, the talented designer and aircraft manufacturer.

In July of the following year Hess became the proud owner of a two-seater monoplane, a BFW (*Bayerische Flugzeugwerke AG*) M23b, serial D-1920, works number 497, which was registered in his name. This light aircraft was donated by the Party newspaper *Völkischer*

*Beobachter*, which had arranged for its name to be painted in large letters on the sides of the fuselage.[13] Hess took great pleasure in flying this machine at very low level above the heads of rival political gatherings. For instance, on 10 August 1930 he spent about two hours circling above an open air meeting of Republicans, making it impossible for the indignant leftists to hear a speech from a visiting Reichstag deputy or to sing their fraternal songs.[14] This resulted in a summons to appear before the Munich police on 23 September. Hess also acquired another BFW M23b, serial D-2043, in May 1931 and a BFW M23c, serial D-1890, the following August.[15] He found time to build up many flying hours in his log book and became a very proficient pilot on light single-engined aircraft.

Meanwhile, in the elections of 1930 the NSDAP became the second strongest party in the Reichstag. Hitler, an Austrian by birth, acquired German citizenship on 24 February 1932 and the NSDAP continued its political progress in the same year. Hess was present at all stages of the party's development and in December 1932 Hitler appointed him Political Central Commissioner of the NSDAP and a delegate to the Reichstag.

Hitler was appointed Chancellor on 30 January 1933 by the German President, Field Marshal Paul von Hindenburg. Hess's devotion was rewarded on 21 April by an appointment as Hitler's deputy. The decree was worded:

> I appoint Party Member Rudolf Hess to be my Deputy, and bestow on him plenary powers to take decisions in my name on all matters affecting the leadership of the Party.[16]

This was followed in December by a further appointment as Minister without Portfolio in the Cabinet. Numerous departments came under his control, including Foreign

Affairs (directed by Joachim von Ribbentrop), Press, Reconstruction, Finance, Law, Germans living abroad (directed by Ernst W. Bohle), Education, Building, Technical matters (directed by Fritz Todt), Health, Race, Art and Literature (directed by Philipp Bouhler). His chief of staff was the notorious Martin Bormann, who was also the *Reichsleiter* (leader) of the Nazi Party and eventually replaced him after the flight to Scotland, as director of the newly created Party Chancellery.

Hess's main office was in the Nazi Headquarters of the Brown House in Munich but there was another bureau under his control in Berlin, known as the *Verbindungstab* (Liaison Staff). This coordinated the activities of the other ministries and was the main channel of communication between the Party and the loose collection of republican States and Provinces that made up the country of Germany. Hitler's long-term strategy was to unify these into a single Fatherland and to achieve supremacy among the world powers, laying the foundation for a Third Reich which would last for a thousand years.

The persecution of the Jews began in April 1933 with the boycott of Jewish businesses and Jews in professional positions. Although Hess was partly responsible for implementing this policy, his attitude towards the Jews was far less virulent than Hitler's. In one instance he ensured that the laws were not effective. Karl Haushofer had married Martha Mayor-Doss, who was half-Jewish, and their two sons Albrecht and Heinz were thus quarter-Jewish. Hess valued his friendship with the family and in June 1933 issued letters which ensured that the two sons came under his protection.[17] In effect, they became 'honorary Aryans', of value to the State. It could be argued that Hess took this action because it suited his purpose, but it is more likely that he was one of the few men among the collection of paranoids and misfits within the Nazi hierarchy who felt some unease at Hitler's extreme policy.

Subsequently, Albrecht became an important adviser to Hess, especially in matters concerning Britain. Born in Munich on 7 January 1903, he entered the city's university at the age of seventeen and read history and geography. He attained his doctor's degree *summa cum laude* four years later, and within the next year became the general secretary for the renowned Society for Geography in Berlin. His travels took him to every country in Europe, the Soviet Union, North and South America, the Near East and the Far East. Politically, he was a cross between a conservative and a liberal, with a hankering for a constitutional monarchy and an intense dislike of revolutionary movements.[18] He loathed Nazism and never joined the NSDAP, and was thus viewed with mistrust and hostility by some members of that movement.

On 2 August 1934 Hindenburg died at the age of nearly eighty-seven, and it seemed from his will and testament that he regarded Hitler as his successor. A plebiscite held on 19 August 1934 resulted in an acceptance of Hitler by about 90 per cent of German voters. The country then began moving towards full dictatorship. During the last day of the 1934 Nuremberg rally, 10 September, Hess shouted to the enormous assembly: 'The Party is Hitler! But Hitler is Germany and Germany is also Hitler! Heil Hitler! Sieg Heil!'

The crowd, in complete ecstasy, roared back its approval: 'Sieg Heil!'

It was an awe-inspiring but terrible experience for those outsiders who witnessed this exhibition of mass hysteria.[19]

Hess's political activities did not hinder his progress with flying. The first national air race, round the Zugspitze Mountain, was planned for 18 February 1934 and he was determined to participate. The contest was postponed twice owing to bad weather. On the second occasion, 10 March, the weather improved slightly but conditions were still variable. The race finally started at

13.30 hours when twelve light aircraft took off from Munich-Oberwiesenfeld airfield and headed for the mountain, 95 km away. Hess, flying a BFW M35, reached the mountain, and was the first to touch down again at the airfield, after a flight of 29 minutes.[20] It was a popular win. On 24 April he was presented with the *Zugspitz-Wanderpokal* (challenge cup) by *Reichsluftsportführer* Bruno Loerzer, an official occasion in which he took immense pride.

The second Zugspitze race took place the following year, deferred by bad weather from 17 to 18 February. On this day the sky was brilliantly clear. Hess was one of the entrants, using the unoriginal pseudonym of Müller and flying a BFW M35b. His navigator was Georg von Wurmb, a flying instructor at the *Deutsche Verkehrsfliegerschule* GmBH (German Commercial Pilots' School) who had been an adjutant for *Jasta 12* in the First World War. On this occasion Hess was not among the winners but came a creditable 6th of the 29 entrants. He received a prize from BFW for the best achievement in flying one of the company's products.[21]

On one occasion in 1936 Hess took off from Berlin's Staaken airfield at the controls of a new Messerschmitt Bf108 *Taifun* (Typhoon) touring aircraft, which first made its appearance in 1934. He performed one manoeuvre after another, not knowing that aerobatics had been temporarily forbidden in this aircraft owing to certain weaknesses that had been discovered in the underside of the fuselage. Hess was informed about the possibility of structural failure after he landed back at the airfield, but his reaction was not recorded.[22]

Hitler's aggressive policies began to alarm the world from 1934. The Saar, which had been lost with the Treaty of Versailles, was returned to Germany following a plebiscite in January 1935. Discontent among German nationals living outside the country was fomented by

Hess's department. These were the dark years when extreme nationalism and false rhetoric triumphed over reason and moderation in Germany, with the Nazis using murder and intimidation as their main weapons while Hess preached the gospel of blind obedience to the Führer. The leaders of the SA, which was considered a threat to Hitler's authority, were rounded up and executed. The movement was suppressed and replaced by the SS, in which Hess had become an *Obergruppenführer* (General in the SS).[23]

Germany marched resolutely along a road which could only end in a Second World War. On 16 March 1935 military conscription was reintroduced. Jews were deprived of citizenship under laws passed the following September. German troops entered the demilitarized Rhineland in March 1936. The Axis of Germany and Italy was formed in October 1936, thus establishing the relationship with the dictator Benito Mussolini. Hitler overhauled the political and military organization of the country on 4 February 1938, forming the *Geheimer Kabinettstrat* (Secret Cabinet Council), of which Hess was made a member. Although Goering denied at the Nuremberg Trials that such a cabinet had even existed, it was established by Hitler to guide him in the conduct of foreign affairs.[24]

The unification with Austria, known as the *Anschluss*, took place in March 1938. Under the terms of the Munich Agreement signed by Hitler, Mussolini and the British and French Prime Ministers, the Sudetenland was ceded to Germany in the following September. During the same year, a wave of anti-semitism swept across Germany. On 7 November a Polish-Jewish youth, Herschel Grynszpan, entered the Germany Embassy in Paris with the intention of killing the Ambassador, Count von Welczek, in revenge for the deportation of his family from their home in Hannover. He was admitted into the office of the Third

Secretary, Ernst vom Rath, drew a revolver and shot him. Vom Rath, who, ironically, opposed anti-semitism, died of his wounds two days later.[25] When the news reached Hitler, he decided to initiate anti-Jewish 'demonstrations'.

The night of 9/10 November was one of despair for Jews living in Germany, for the police remained passive during an orgy of destruction and horror. Jews were murdered or beaten and arrested, while their houses were burnt or their shops wrecked and the contents thrown on the streets. The broken glass in the streets gave rise to the name *Kristallnacht* (night of broken glass). Hess, less of a hard-liner on the subject of Jews, was appalled. He did not agree with ill-treatment or the plundering of businesses. His reaction came in the form of a notice sent from his office to all *Gauleiters* (provincial governors), requiring them to cease immediately 'burning Jewish businesses and the like'[26] (see Appendix A). Of course, the outside world decided that Germany had become a barbaric country. Some Germans were also outraged and Hess, who was especially dejected, asked Hitler to stop the pogrom.

In March 1939 German troops invaded Czechoslovakia in defiance of the Munich Agreement, and in the same month Memel in Lithuania was ceded to Germany. At the end of the month the British Prime Minister Neville Chamberlain announced an Anglo-French guarantee of the boundaries of Poland in the event of German aggression; this vain attempt to thwart Hitler's further ambitions increased dramatically the prospect of war. Germany signed a non-aggression pact with Russia in August 1939, to the dismay of the Western Powers.

Hess participated in all these events, although he was in the wings rather than on centre stage. He was sometimes known behind his back as the 'brown mouse'. Nevertheless he was a popular figure among the German public, partly for his war record but primarily for his unquestioning loyalty to Hitler. He was portrayed as the ideal to which every citizen should aspire. Hess revelled in this popularity, but his world was soon to fall apart.

At 20.00 hours on Thursday 31 August 1939 *SS-Sturmbahnführer* (Major) Alfred Helmut Naujocks looked at his wristwatch, waiting for the moment. He and his small force were outside the German radio station at Gleiwitz in Upper Silesia, some 135 km east-south-east of Breslau. Clad in Polish uniforms, the *SD-Sonderkommando* (SD-Special Detachment) stormed inside, firing shots in the air. Those on duty were put under lock and key, guarded by one of the raiders. A German interpreter grabbed the microphone and shouted in Polish:

Attention! Attention! This is the Polish Freedom Committee. The radio station Gleiwitz is in our hands. The hour of freedom has arrived . . . the cities of Danzig and Breslau will be Polish again!

A few minutes later, the raiding party left the building and vanished. At 04.45 hours on 1 September 1939, Germany invaded Poland. Two days later, Britain and France were at war with Germany.

# CHAPTER THREE

## *Preparations for the Flight*

Soon after the German invasion of Poland, Hess asked Hitler for permission to join the Luftwaffe and take part in the air operations. Of course, Hitler refused and forbade him to fly an aircraft for the duration of the war. Hess replied that this was too severe a prohibition and asked if it was possible to limit the term to a single year. To his surprise, Hitler agreed, probably thinking that Hess would have forgotten his enthusiasm by the end of this period and that the war could be over in any event. Nothing was further from the truth.

Before making his request, Hess had been relegated from his position in the Nazi hierarchy. On the day of the invasion of Poland, Hitler addressed the nation from the Reichstag. His speech was the usual tirade of abuse and lies but he did make one statement of significance. He named Field Marshal Hermann Goering, the Commander-in-Chief of the Luftwaffe and former war hero, as his successor in the event of his death, with Hess next in line. Hess's position was further eroded when Hitler appointed Martin Bormann as his private secretary. In fact he was continuously sidelined as the war progressed, with the conquest of Poland, the 'phoney war' with Britain and France from 3 September 1939 to April 1940, the conquest of Denmark and Norway from 9 April 1940, and the successful Blitzkrieg in the West which resulted in France's capitulation on 25 June 1940.

This was the time when Hess contemplated bringing off a dramatic coup by achieving peace with England, as a

'Parliamentary on his own initiative'. However, it is not generally known that he was not the first Nazi leader to conceive such an idea. In *A Record of Events before the War, 1939*, written in diary form by Lord Halifax, the British Foreign Secretary from February 1938 to December 1940, the following entry appears for Monday 21 August 1939:

'C' [Admiral Sir Hugh 'Quex' Sinclair, head of MI6] tells us that he has received an approach suggesting that Goering should come to London if he can be assured that he will be able to see the Prime Minister. It was decided to send an affirmative answer to this curious suggestion, and arrangements were accordingly set in hand for Goering to come over secretly on Wednesday the 23rd. The idea is that he should land at some deserted aerodrome [Bovington in Hertfordshire according to one source], be picked up in a car and taken direct to Chequers [the country house of the Prime Minister, in Buckinghamshire]. There the regular household is to be given congé and the telephone is to be disconnected. It looks as though it is going to be a dramatic interlude and, having laid the plans, we await confirmation from Germany.[1]

On the following day there was still no news of Goering's visit. Twelve days later Lord Halifax records: 'I did not see that there was any good in Goering coming here.'[2]

By September 1940 Hess was considering making peace overtures to Britain, apparently with Hitler's knowledge, and sought the advice of Albrecht Haushofer for suitable contacts in the enemy country.[3] After considering many names, he chose the unsuspecting Duke of Hamilton, a man who had developed friendly relations with Albrecht during the latter's pre-war visits to Britain. The premier peer of Scotland, Hamilton was aged thirty-eight and had succeeded to the dukedom on the death of his father in March 1940. As the former Marquis of Clydesdale he had been a Member of Parliament for Renfrewshire East for ten years. He was also an aviator who served in the Royal Auxiliary Air Force, commanding 602 (City of Glasgow) Squadron from 1927 to 1937. He had been the first pilot in the modified Westland PV-3 that made the first successful flight over Everest in 1933, a feat for which he had been awarded the Air Force Cross. Known as 'Douglo' to his fellow officers, Hamilton was respected as a modest and unassuming man in spite of his high position in society and proficiency as a pilot.

Hamilton and Hess had never met nor had any connection with each other, although both had attended a banquet during the Olympic Games held in Berlin in August 1936, when they sat at different tables.[4] Hess thought, quite mistakenly, that he would find in Hamilton an ally in his search for peace between the two countries. He had somehow conceived the totally erroneous idea that Hamilton was a member of a party which opposed the government led by Winston Churchill and had the special ear of the king. He also believed that there would be some empathy between them since both were accomplished pilots who had achieved international recognition.

On 23 September 1940 Albrecht wrote to Hamilton, with Hess's agreement, sending the letter via Lisbon and suggesting that they should meet in that city. This letter was intercepted by MI5 and not shown to Hamilton until March 1941. No positive action was taken about the proposed meeting before Hess made his unexpected flight to Scotland.[5]

Meanwhile Hess resumed his efforts to train in the latest German warplanes. In the middle of September he went to Berlin-Tempelhof airfield to visit the celebrated pilot *Generaloberst* Ernst Udet, who at the time was *Generalluftzeugmeister* (Chief of Aircraft Supply).[6] He asked if Udet could supply a Messerschmitt Bf110 twin-engined 'destroyer' for some occasional practice flying. When Udet reminded him of his promise to Hitler, Hess replied that the ban had been for only a year, which had now expired. Thus Udet agreed to the request, but on the proviso that Hitler signed a permit. Hess knew that this would never be granted and abandoned his enquiry.

A few days after this refusal Hess visited some factories where Messerschmitt Bf109 single-engined fighters were being assembled. This machine did not have the range to reach Scotland, but Hess may have considered some modifications which would enable it to do so. The Germans were well aware that long-range Spitfires, stripped of their armament and fitted with extra internal fuel tanks, were being employed by the RAF for photo-reconnaissance. One had been captured intact at Coulomniers in France during the Blitzkrieg while others had been shot down over Germany and the Low Countries. The latest variant, introduced in October 1940 and known as the Spitfire PR ID or the 'flying petrol bowser', could fly for about 1,750 miles. Half that distance in a modified Bf109 would be sufficient for Hess on a one-way flight to Scotland.

However, at the *Wiener-Neustädter-Flugzeugwerke* chief test pilot Knut emphatically refused Hess's request to fly one of these machines. One possible reason for his reluctance was that the Bf109 could be a dangerous aircraft in the hands of a newcomer to the type. The undercarriage was weak and had a narrow track, so that the machine was prone to 'ground loops' during taxying, take-off and especially landing. As a result Bf109s were damaged at an alarming rate in this early part of the war, with 255 accidents in 1939 alone. The main fault was in the castoring of the tailwheel, which was eventually remedied by the introduction of a lock.[7] No one who valued his own well-being would wish to endanger the life of Hitler's

*Stellvertreter* (Deputy). Hess then tried the Arado factory in Warnemünde but received a similar refusal from chief test pilot Schniring. At the Fieseler factory in Kassel his request was turned down by Gerhard Fieseler.

By now almost at the end of his tether, Hess went to Augsburg to see his old friend Willy Messerschmitt, in the hope that he would be able to help. This was the factory where the Bf108 touring aircraft and the Bf109 fighter had been built, although in the summer of that year production of these single-engined machines had been transferred to Messerschmitt's other factory at Regensburg. Production of the twin-engined Bf110 continued at Augsburg, although it was also being built elsewhere under licence. Air-testing of these Bf110s took place at the Augsburg-Haunstetten airfield. By this time, Hess knew that flying the difficult Bf109 was out of the question and he asked if he could fly the Bf110 instead. To his relief, Willy raised no objectives. There were probably several reasons for this agreement. First, he seems to have owed Hess a debt of honour. In 1932 the city of Augsburg had announced its intention of acquiring this factory as a depot for tramcars, and it is believed that Hess used his influence to thwart this proposal to oust Willy from his own premises. Secondly, Willy knew that Hess was a competent and experienced pilot on single-engined machines and that his conversion on to twin-engined and heavier aircraft should be quite easy. Thirdly, since the Bf110 was a two-seater, an instructor could accompany Hess on his initial flights, after teaching him the intricacies of the controls on the ground. Then he would be able to fly solo.[8]

In October 1940 Hess began training in the Bf110, instructed by the chief test pilot at the Messerschmitt Works, Willi Stoer. A former pilot at the *Deutsche Verkehrsfliegerschule* (German Commercial Pilots' School), Stoer had won the German aerobatic championships twice, in 1935 and 1936, at the controls of a BFW M35. At first, he demonstrated the Bf110 while sitting in the pilot's seat with Hess occupying the observer/wireless operator/gunner's seat behind. Another test pilot was Helmut Kaden, who took over Stoer's position when the latter was posted to Japan on 4 May 1941. Before his death on 26 February 1992, *Flugkapitän a.D* Kaden corresponded at length with both the authors of this book, providing numerous details as well as copies of sections of his pilot's log book that related to Hess. According to Kaden, Stoer flew with Hess on five occasions before they changed places, and the two men then flew together on five more flights before it became clear to Stoer that his pupil was ready to fly solo. Some other sources state that Hess flew ten times at the controls before Stoer allowed him to take off on his own. The exact number cannot be verified since the Messerschmitt factory at Augsburg was heavily bombed by B-17 Flying Fortresses of the U.S. Eighth Air Force on 25 February 1944 and 13 April 1944.[9] Kaden stated that most of the logs of the control tower were destroyed in those raids.[10] In any event, all went well with Hess's flights and he became a regular visitor to the airfield, mostly on Saturday mornings.

On 4 November 1940 Hess wrote a short but enigmatic letter from Berlin to his wife Ilse. It read:

I firmly believe that from the flight I am about to make one of these days, I will return and the flight will be crowned with success. However, if not, the goal I have set myself will have been worth the supreme effort. I know that all of you understand me; you will know that I could not have acted otherwise. [See Appendix B]

It is apparent from this letter that Hess had finally made up his mind to fly to Britain, in the absence of any reply to Albrecht Haushofer's letter of 23 September to Hamilton. He knew that Hamilton lived at Dungavel House near

Glasgow, and this became his objective, despite the distance from Augsburg. However, at this stage he needed much more experience with the Bf110. After a period of practising solo take-offs, circuits and landings, he began cross-country flights. He also flew a number of different Bf110s, after each had come off the production line and been air tested by the Messerschmitt pilots. These machines were usually tested over a period of about a fortnight. After completion of this programme, they were placed on a 'delivery availability' list of the *Bauaufsicht-Luft* (Building-Inspectorate-Air, or BAL).[11] These available aircraft were stored in a *Luftpark* (Aircraft Storage Depot), one of which was at Lechfeld, south of Augsburg. It is known that Hess made a number of short visits to this depot, and he was probably able to take his pick of the machines.

Exact details of Hess's cross-country flights are not available, although several attempts have been made to list some of the later ones. Of these various sources, probably the most authoritative is Helmut Kaden, who was closely concerned with them at the time and was also responsible for the preparation of Hess's aircraft.[12] With hindsight, Kaden believed that some of the flights were genuine attempts to fly to Scotland, but that they were aborted for various reasons. To some extent this belief was supported by Hess himself, for on arrival in Britain he stated that his flight was his third attempt to fly to Scotland.[13] Later, however, he admitted that the first genuine attempt was when he made his historic flight on 10 May 1941.[14] It is the belief of the authors of this book that the earlier cross-country flights were no more than 'dummy runs' during which Hess tested various items of equipment, checked his ability to fly steadily for a long period, and familiarized himself with the landscape on the first part of his route. Any prudent pilot would have found such flights advisable before making a genuine attempt. (See Appendix C)

It is also known, primarily from Helmut Kaden, that Hess had a number of amiable chats with various test pilots at the airfield after returning from each flight. Of course, these men were flattered to receive attention from such an eminent person as the Deputy Führer and they responded eagerly to his questions. At first these were of a general and innocent nature but over the months they became more technical and probing: 'Is it possible to install an automatic pilot in the cockpit?' 'Can the wireless set mounted in the rear for use by the observer/wireless operator/gunner be moved to the pilot's cockpit?' In fact it was simple to install the automatic pilot but technically impossible to shift the wireless set, although a modification could be devised which would enable the pilot to operate it from his cockpit. On another occasion Hess complained that the machine he was flying at the time was fitted with an old-type heater with no cut-off valve between it and the radiator.[15]

According to Kaden, when Hess landed one day he commented that the machine he had just flown was very much to his liking. It was well known among wartime aviators that aircraft could develop different characteristics, even if they came off the same production line. Some had strange quirks but others were more responsive and the engines ran sweetly. The machine Hess favoured was a Bf110E-1/N, radio code VJ+OQ, works number 3869. Production of this machine was completed on 21 November 1940 and it was then flown by test pilots who cannot be identified since the records were destroyed in the American bombing raids. However, it is known that it was held in the *Luftpark* some time before the end of December 1940.[16] Hess asked if this machine could be held in reserve for his personal use. This presented no problem and from then on he never flew another Bf110.[17]

On another visit to the airfield, Hess noticed that Kaden was about to take off in a Bf110 fitted with two huge drop-tanks, larger than those he had seen before, each containing 900 litres of fuel. He must have understood the significance of these tanks, for they would increase his aircraft's range sufficiently to reach Dungavel House, and he asked if a set could be provided for his personal aircraft. Once again, there was no problem and the tanks were fitted whenever he wanted to make a long-distance flight.[18] Sometimes his flights took him from Augsburg towards Kiel and over the Thüringer Forest, a mountainous region in central Germany with heights ranging from 600 to 982 metres.[19] Flying over such a terrain gave him the necessary experience before making a flight over the similar border regions of Northumberland and Scotland.

Another installation in his aircraft was a radio compass, and Hess was anxious to ensure that this could pick up the transmitting station near Kalundborg in Denmark, which happened to be on the same latitude as Dungavel House in Scotland.

Hess's senior adjutant was Lieutenant Karlheinz Pintsch, aged thirty-one, who accompanied him to Augsburg on these occasions and awaited his return from each flight. According to the author James Leasor, who interviewed Pintsch before his book about Hess was published in 1962, two sealed letters were handed to Pintsch when the Bf110 was being prepared for a flight in January 1941. One was addressed to Hitler and the other to Pintsch himself. Hess told him to open his personal letter if he did not return in four hours and take the other to Hitler. In the event, this time elapsed and Pintsch learned that Hess intended to fly to Scotland in an attempt to make peace with Britain.[20] If this happened, as seems very feasible from a later German announcement, Pintsch maintained secrecy until Hess's final flight.

On 29 March 1941 Helmut Kaden began a series of air tests with Hess's personal machine. Meanwhile Hess asked if the four oxygen bottles mounted in the fuselage to supply the observer could be interconnected for use by the pilot, thus doubling his own supply of oxygen. This was done, although there were then two mouthpieces in his cockpit.[21] He asked for a number of other technical alterations during Kaden's tests. There were five of these tests, with an average duration of 15 minutes, the last being on 6 May with the wireless operator Josef Blümel. Unknown to Kaden, the Bf110 was then ready for the flight to Scotland. (See Appendix D)

Another matter which occupied Hess's attention for many months was the weather. From the autumn of 1940, his secretary Hildegard Fath received regular phone calls. A voice at the other end gave her the weather conditions for three locations, identified by the letters X, Y and Z. Hess never disclosed the geographical location of these symbols and it is unlikely that they were known to Hildegard Fath. This matter has confused many other authors, who have made various assumptions and drawn different conclusions from the mystery.[22] In 1993 one of the authors of this book made contact, via official sources, with one of the nine meteorologists who worked in the former *Zentrale Wetterdienst Gruppe* (ZWG or Central Weather Group) at Potsdam-Wildpark and were responsible for providing daily weather forecasts to Hess up to the time of his flight to Scotland.[23] This was Dr 'F.S.', an eminent meteorologist who, at the age of eighty-five in 1993, wrote to the authors in German. He asked us not to identify him, for he preferred to keep well clear of matters which might be regarded as political in Germany, but a translation of part of his letter is as follows:

Every day round 10.00 am, we [at the ZWG] received a telephone call from Rudolf Hess's secretary asking for the weather forecasts for the triangle formed by the cities Oslo-Kiel-Edinburgh (i.e. Oslo = X, Kiel = Y and Z = Edinburgh).

The meteorologist on duty prepared a summary, making it comprehensible to the person on the other end of the telephone. This went on for several months until the voice at the other end said 'Thank you very much, gentlemen, from tomorrow my boss no longer needs your information!' Why Rudolf Hess took so much interest in the weather over the North Sea was of no concern to us. We were only too glad to get rid of this little daily obligation. The next day, around noon, we heard that Hess had flown to Scotland, making it abundantly clear to us why he had needed our daily weather reports for several months.

Normally, a pilot asked a meteorologist for a weather report concerning his flight route but, if Hess had done this, we meteorologists would have had knowledge of his intentions. It became known later that he had taken off from Augsburg-Haunstetten airfield.

Dr 'F.S.' was of the opinion that these weather reports would have enabled Hess to anticipate conditions over the North Sea. Of course, since Hess was one of the top members of the Nazi hierarchy, the information was given readily and no questions were asked. During the war weather forecasts were *Streng Geheim* (most secret) in Germany, as they were in all the belligerent nations, and not accessible to the general public. They were of prime importance for military operations and were never disclosed to the enemy. All countries created units devoted to weather reports and in Germany these were known as *Wettererkundungsstaffeln* (Meteorological Reconnaissance Squadrons). Since the prevailing weather fronts arrived from the west, the daily missions of the German aircraft could be dangerous, flying towards the enemy before bringing back information for the bomber groups.

Our informant, Dr 'F.S.', served with the Condor Legion in Spain and later flew with *Wekusta 26*, which was stationed at Grimbergen, near Brussels, from September 1940 to April 1941. He survived many sorties over England and sent us a graphic account of his experiences. We are grateful to him for clearing up a mystery which has baffled researchers over the years.[24]

In addition to obtaining the latest weather reports, Hess gathered together a number of personal items. He took with him ten Reichsmark notes and the visiting cards of Dr Albrecht Haushofer and Dr Karl Haushofer, with the intention of presenting the latter to the Duke of Hamilton.[25] He collected a Leica camera, a small electric torch, a safety razor blade and a hypodermic syringe sterilized in alcohol. In addition he carried with him a selection of twenty-eight medicines in small tin cases, boxes, tubes and bottles. These included methylbenzedrine for preventing sleep, barbiturates for inducing sleep, opiates for dulling pain and atropine tablets which were probably intended for alleviating air sickness. There were also tablets containing ingredients such as dextrose, kola and lecithin for reducing the effects of fatigue. In addition there were pills and tablets containing homeopathic medication. This collection was later analysed by the British Medical Research Council and found to be fairly harmless in the quantities carried.[26] It was considered evidence of hypochondria, a defect that seems to have plagued Hess in spite of a remarkably robust constitution which enabled him to recover from several wounds and to survive for so many years. However, he neglected to take a change of underwear with him, indicating either that he anticipated a short stay in Britain or that he expected his hosts would provide him with such necessities.

Hess's last public appearance took place on Germany's

National Labour Day, 1 May 1941, when he deputized for Hitler by delivering a speech at the Messerschmitt Works in Augsburg, in honour of the country's 'model factories' and of three men on whom had been bestowed the title 'Pioneer of Labour'. These were Max Amman, *Reichsleiter* for the Press, Dr Ohnesorge, Minister of Posts, and Dr Willy Messerschmitt.[27]

Saturday 10 May 1941 promised to be a beautiful day in Munich, with a temperature of between 5 and 6 degrees Centigrade in the early hours and variable winds. It would be warm and sunny around noon but cloud was expected later in the day.[28] The Hess family lived in affluent circumstances at 48 Harthauser Strasse, München-Harlaching. Ilse had noticed that Rudolf was spending more time with their son Wolf Rüdiger than usual. She had no explanation for this but later understood his behaviour: he was tormented by the thought that he might never see again the three-and-a-half year old boy, whom he affectionately nicknamed 'Buz'.[29] In the morning, he took Buz for a stroll along the right bank of the River Isar and then they visited the nearby Hellabrun Zoo. Of course, the little boy could not have been aware that he would never walk beside his father again. In fact the next time he would see him would be in Spandau prison on 24 December 1969.

The two of them returned about noon, for Hess was expecting a visitor for luncheon. This was Alfred Rosenberg, the Party ideologist who was to be appointed by Hitler as Reichs Minister for the Eastern Occupied Territories on 17 July 1941.[30] He arrived punctually and was shown in by the butler. Hess welcomed his visitor and the two men went into the dining-room for a luncheon of cold meats. Ilse was not feeling well and remained in her room, while Hess had given instructions to his household staff that he and his visitor were not to be disturbed under any circumstances. There is thus no record of their conversation and it remains a mystery to this day. It is known, however, that Rosenberg left about an hour afterwards and went straight to the Berghof, where Hitler was staying at the time.[31] Some writers have assumed that he delivered a report to the Führer about Hess's imminent departure and thus Hitler knew and approved of his intentions.[32] However, there is no evidence to support this contention. It is quite possible, for instance, that the subject under discussion was the forthcoming attack by Germany on Russia. As is now known, as early as July 1940 Hitler had ordered his military commanders to prepare for this great assault that was to begin in May 1941.[33] By the time Hess made his flight, British military intelligence was aware, from decrypts of enemy 'Enigma' signals as well as from information from underground and neutral sources, of the enormous build-up of the Wehrmacht along the borders of Russian-held territory. It became clear later that the attack would not take place until after 15 June.[34] In fact, operation 'Barbarossa' began on 22 June.

After his guest left, Hess took a short rest and in mid afternoon went up to Ilse's room to join her for a cup of tea. His wife was surprised to see him dressed elegantly in a blue-grey uniform with the rank insignia of a *Hauptman* (Captain) in the Luftwaffe, high boots and a dark blue tie on a blue shirt. She had asked him for several years to wear this combination of tie and shirt but up to then he had refused. On asking why he had chosen to wear them, she was delighted when he smiled and replied: 'To make you happy!'[35]

Hess had already told Ilse that he had received a telephone call ordering him to Berlin, but that first he had to make a detour via Augsburg.[36] There are no records to substantiate his statement, and it is more likely that the call had been made by himself to Haunstetten airfield, ordering his personal aircraft to be prepared for a flight. This was always parked under guard in one of the hangars, ready for his use.[37] After fourteen years of marriage and watching his moods, Ilse probably knew intuitively that something strange was afoot. The extra attention to their son, the calls giving weather reports, maps on his bedroom wall, a brand-new radio always tuned into Kalundborg in Denmark and his frequent visits to Augsburg must have aroused her curiosity. She asked:

'When you are coming back?'

'I don't know exactly,' was his reply. 'Maybe by tomorrow, but certainly by Monday evening at the latest.'

'Tomorrow? Monday evening? I don't believe you'll be back so soon.'[38]

Before she could question him further, Hess said goodbye and left hastily. The time was around 15.30 hours. His large official car was awaiting him, probably a Mercedes-Benz type 770KW150 (although this cannot be verified), with his driver Rudolf Lippert at the wheel. Hess was accompanied by his adjutant Lieutenant Karlheinz Pintsch, his personal orderly Jozef Platzer and his security guard Franz Lutz.[39] It was a drive of about an hour through the outskirts of Munich and along the highway to the airfield.

According to one source, Hess was running a little early for his planned time of take-off and stopped for half an hour before reaching Haunstetten; he and Pintsch went for a stroll through the Bavarian mountain crocuses.[40] In any event the Mercedes eventually arrived at the airfield, where the sentries saluted Hess and opened the gates. Contrary to statements in other books, the airfield was not deserted. Test flying went on from early morning until sunset (18.30 hours at this time) on every day of the week, including Saturdays and Sundays.[41] They drove to the apron where the Bf110 was standing, its internal tanks and huge drop-tanks filled to capacity. The airport manager Piel, chief test pilot Kaden and several mechanics were waiting for the party.

Followed by Pintsch, Hess went to Kaden's office where he made a last telephone call, probably to the meteorological office at Hamburg. Both men then entered the changing room, where Hess donned a black leather flying suit belonging to Kaden and a pair of fleece-lined flying boots. He emerged carrying his oxygen mask and dark brown, fleece-lined flying helmet, while Pintsch carried his seat parachute. After being helped into his parachute harness, Hess put on his helmet and shook hands with those present. He climbed up the boarding ladder, stepped on the wingroot and clambered into the cockpit of his aircraft. Once inside, he was strapped into his seat by Kaden and he then clipped the oxygen mask to his helmet. Before closing the side windows and cockpit roof, Kaden tapped him lightly on the head, saying 'Hals – und Beinbruch!' ('Break your neck and leg!')[42]

As with all other military aircraft, there was a standard procedure for starting the Bf110. The pilot first switched on the electrical system and ensured that the undercarriage selector was switched to 'down' and locked. He checked that the flying instruments were operating correctly, set the altimeter to height above mean sea level, and ensured that all the flying controls were moving freely. The fuel cocks were then switched to 'on', the propeller pitches set to 'fine' and the throttles opened three-quarters. All his checks complete, Hess pressed the starter button for the port engine and it came to life with a loud roar, emitting clouds of bluish-white smoke from the exhausts. Next the starter button of the starboard engine was pressed and more clouds of smoke filled the air. Both engines were run up at low speed for about a minute and then opened up to about 1,000 rpm, while the magnetos were checked for any drop in revolutions. Then both engines were throttled back and the hand signal 'Chocks away!' was given. The mechanics pulled on the ropes and the heavy chocks came away from in front of the wheels. With a sudden burst of power from the two Daimler-Benz DB601N engines, the Bf110 rolled out from its hard-standing. The brakes squealed as the heavy machine turned to taxi towards the end of the grass runway, which at Augsburg-Haunstetten was 1,100 metres long and 50 metres wide. At the end of the runway, the brakes squealed again as the pilot brought the machine to a halt and checked his instruments once more. The flaps were set at 20 degrees. At this stage, the fuel was always switched to the main tanks.

Hess called the control tower on his radio telephone and received an immediate clearance for take off. The machine hesitated for a brief moment while the pilot pushed the throttles fully forward. With the propellers set at fine pitch, the engines gave an ear-shattering roar which penetrated the interior of the aircraft and the earphones of the pilot's helmet. The machine vibrated as the rapid acceleration pressed the pilot back into his seat. He raised the tail quite quickly and corrected any tendency to swing with the rudder.[43] The run itself was quite lengthy but eventually the pilot pulled back gently on the control column and the machine lifted smoothly off the runway. The control column was pushed forward again to gain speed. The flaps were reset and the wheels of the undercarriage retracted into their wells while the doors closed slowly. Soon afterwards, the pilot began transferring fuel from the drop-tanks into the main tanks.

Hess gained altitude, made a wide turn east of the River Lech, climbed in a north-westerly direction and eventually disappeared from sight. He had taken off at precisely 17.45 hours German Summer Time.[44]

# CHAPTER FOUR

## *The Flight*

For several months Hess had been poring over maps of north-west Europe, the boundaries of the North Sea, the northern sector of Northumberland and the south of Scotland. He had been living in a world of aircraft instruments, piston pressures, cooling water temperatures, oxygen supplies, detachable fuel tanks, auxiliary oil pumps, aircraft performance figures, radio bearings, synoptic charts and all the other details that are studied by aircrew preparatory to a long-distance flight. In his case, however, he had been compelled to compile the information by surreptitious means, whereas operational airmen were always briefed by a succession of different specialists. Now he was on his way at last, convinced that the most important mission of his life would succeed. The German weather forecast was favourable, indicating a large anti-cyclone to the west of Britain, with light westerly winds over Germany and the Low Countries veering to northerly over the North Sea. Cloud was scattered and visibility was good. Unknown to Hess, the British synoptic chart at 14.00 hours local time was quite similar, although probably more accurate to the west of Britain, where it showed the large anti-cyclone over the North Atlantic preceded by a weak cold front. This British forecast indicated light variable winds over north-east England and south-west Scotland, where conditions were expected to be mainly cloudy with a few showers, perhaps of a thundery type.[1] Hess had chosen an excellent day.

It is possible to reconstruct the latter part of his flight

from RAF sources, but the earlier part is best described in a long letter he wrote some time between 10 and 15 June 1941, while in captivity, to his son 'Buz'.[2] Hess was justifiably proud of his skill in making the solo flight, but he must have been aware that a boy of less than four years old would not be able to read the letter, let alone fully understand its content. Of course he knew that the letter would be read aloud to the boy by his wife Ilse, who might also pass the information on to those competent to understand his methods and admire his achievement, such as the pilots in the Messerschmitt Works. Even if Ilse kept the information to herself for the time being, Hess was recording his flight for prosperity.

After mentioning his smooth take-off and a wide sweep east of the River Lech, he described setting a course of 320 degrees towards Bonn. At first he could not identify anything on the ground to check his position, but eventually a railway junction verified that he was exactly on track. Darmstadt loomed up later on his starboard, giving him another pinpoint. Some time afterwards he spotted the point where the River Main flows into the Rhine. By then he was a few degrees off track and made a minor adjustment of course on the automatic pilot. The Rhine disappeared to his port, but reappeared eventually. By this time, he could see the Siebengebirge (Seven Mountains) in the distance and the spa town of Bad Godesberg in Westphalia, south-east of Bonn. He said that these brought back childhood memories, as well as recollections of staying there with the Führer, and his last visit when the fall of France was imminent.[3]

From Bonn he altered course to 335 degrees. This took him near the town of Haldern, some 34 km from the German–Dutch border, from where the Rhine sweeps towards the west and could no longer be used as a guide. He continued on the same course, near Arnhem and then over the IJsselmeer (more generally known outside the

Netherlands as the Zuider Zee). This track must have taken him between the Dutch Frisian islands of Vlieland and Terschelling, providing excellent pinpoints. He commented that he found a bright sky, whereas the German forecast had indicated cloudy conditions.[4]

He then turned and flew for 23 minutes in a generally easterly direction. Although in his letter he says that this was against the wind, the German synoptic chart in this area indicates a light north-westerly wind. The purpose of this change of direction was probably to keep clear of the British radar system, which had been so effective in the Battle of Britain. He then turned on to a heading of 335 degrees for his long journey over the North Sea. At 20.10 hours German Summer Time, when part of the way along this leg, he flew over two German U-boats, which began to dive but then remained on the surface when they recognized the aircraft as friendly.[5] These U-boats were probably en route to or returning from the North Atlantic, where they were extremely active at this time in combination with Focke-Wulfe Fw200 Kondor long-distance bombers. It is clear that Hess was at a fairly low altitude at this point, since both he and the look-outs in the conning towers were able to recognize each other as friendly. However, shortly afterwards he climbed to the more economical altitude of 5,000 metres, where the outside temperature was minus 26 degrees Centigrade. He was still beyond the range of British radar stations, but his aircraft could possibly be picked up by German radar stations situated in Denmark.

It was around this time that alarm bells began to ring in Germany. In his autobiography, the celebrated fighter ace Adolf Galland, who at the time was a *Oberstleutnant* (Lieutenant-Colonel) commanding a Fighter Group on the Channel coast, recalls how he received a highly agitated telephone call from *Reichsmarschall* Goering in the early evening of 10 May 1941, ordering him to take off with his entire Group. When Galland pointed out that there were no reports of enemy aircraft flying towards Germany and that it was getting dark, Goering replied that the Deputy Führer had gone mad, was flying to Britain in a Bf110, and must be shot down.

Galland asked for the probable course of the machine and then put down the receiver, wondering who had gone mad – Hess, Goering or himself. Knowing nothing about Hess's special machine, he thought it unlikely that he would reach his destination, and if even he reached Scotland he would probably be shot down by Spitfires. He knew that many other Bf110s would be in the air, on training flights or air tests preparatory to operational sorties. How could his pilots pick out Hess's machine? As a sop to Goering, he ordered each squadron commander to send up a couple of fighters to fly around for a while, without telling them why and knowing that they would think he had gone off his head. Of course, he had to report failure to Goering.[6]

It is not clear how the *Reichsmarschall* became aware of Hess's destination. Hess had left a letter with his adjutant Karlheinz Pintsch, addressed to Hitler and announcing his intention of flying to Britain. Hitler was staying at the Berghof, his Bavarian mountain retreat in Berchtesgaden, but this letter did not reach him until the following morning. It seems that Pintsch had also been instructed by Hess to ensure that radio direction signals were available to help his navigation towards Scotland, and Goering was informed.

Ignoring any fury he might have left behind, Hess continued on exactly the same course. It seems possible that he was able to check his latitude by tuning his radio compass to a bearing from the German transmitting station *Kastanie Y*, near Kalundborg in Denmark, since this station had interested him for the past few months, both at home and on his cross-country flights from

Augsburg. In any event, he continued flying until, in his own words, he arrived at the *Nordpunkt* (North Point) at about 20.58 hours and then turned to port on a course of 245 degrees towards the *Punkt B* (Point B) marked on his map near the little coastal town of Bamburgh in Northumberland.

He had made several marks with chinagraph pencils on two of his maps. Railways and other prominent landmarks were emphasized while the Duke of Hamilton's home, Dungavel House near Glasgow, was picked out with a red arrow pointing towards a small reservoir nearby. He had also written in pencil the words *Küste zu Küste* (coast to coast) as well as the words *Peilung* (bearing) and '*Inseln* (islands) – Cheviot 255 degrees'. The islands were Holy Island and the Farne Islands, and the bearing must have referred to the Luftwaffe's transmitting stations in northern Denmark. There were several of these on the reciprocal of this bearing, such as *Schakal* (Jackal) at Skagen, *Jasmin-Y* (Jasmine) at Tornby/Hjörring and *Hyäne* (Hyena) at Lyngby. It would have made navigational sense to use one of these radio stations to determine his northern turning point. He later told his wife that he could not obtain these bearings,[7] but this must have been a legitimate ruse to persuade the British that his radio compass was not effective.

Two of Hess's maps, stuck together, are now on public display behind glass at Lennoxlove, near Haddington in East Lothian, the home of the present Duke of Hamilton. They are topographical maps on a scale of 1:250,000 covering the north of England and the south of Scotland, the whole measuring 126 by 79 cm. A third map covering the area to the north is not on display. All appear to be part of a series prepared for aerial map-reading by the British Ordnance Survey, with the place names in English but the legend in German. They were presented to the Duke's father by the Air Ministry, together with Hess's camera and hand compass. The camera was returned to Frau Hess many years ago, but the compass is still on display.[8]

Hess flew on this course of 245 degrees for 20 minutes. However, although the sun was low in the sky, the light was still far too bright for safety. It seems probable that he had underestimated the time of sunset in this northerly latitude and that the sky was less cloudy than he expected from the German weather forecast. He turned and flew in a reciprocal direction, then alternated between 065 and 245 degrees for about 40 minutes to await the approaching darkness.[9] After using up time in this way, he resumed his westerly course. At some stage during these manoeuvres, the fuel in his drop-tanks must have become exhausted, as he had been transferring it into the main tanks for several hours. He then released the drop-tanks into the sea, to reduce drag on the aircraft for a high-speed approach.

At about this time the RAF's Fighter Command became aware of the intruder. There were twenty-two Chain Home (CH) or Chain Home Low (CHL) radar stations around the coasts of Britain, and their reports of enemy aircraft were passed instantly to Fighter Command's headquarters at Bentley Priory in Middlesex. Blips of enemy aircraft on each cathode-ray screen could be distinguished from RAF aircraft since the latter carried an instrument known as IFF (Identification Friend or Foe). The system was not perfect, however, and it was the duty of the Filter Room at Bentley Priory to confirm whether a report was likely to be friendly or enemy. The first report of an approaching enemy came in at 22.08 hours, soon after sunset, from the CH station at Ottercops Moss, north-west of Newcastle-upon-Tyne, which identified it as 'three plus aircraft travelling almost due west at a speed of approximately 300 mph' (see Appendix E). If Hess's recollection of his times is accurate, his aircraft was identified by radar 16 minutes after he had finished flying to and fro and had begun his final leg to the coast of Northumberland.

A single coloured counter was placed near Holy Island on the plotting table map in the Filter Room, distinguishing it from those counters which denoted friendly aircraft. On the counter was an arrow indicating direction as well as numerals showing altitude and strength. Overlooking the table were three young aircraftwomen, known as 'tellers', whose duty it was to watch these counters and report their progress to an officer in the adjoining Operations Room, who in turn issued orders to the RAF fighter stations. The teller allocated to this 'raid' was Corporal Felicity Ashbee, who later rose to the rank of flight officer. She remembers the occasion vividly. The three girls laughed quietly for a few moments, since Ottercops Moss was situated in a remote and hilly area which made radar readings rather difficult and its operators had a reputation for getting thunderstorms mixed up with aircraft blips on the radar screens. However, other reports soon came in from Danby Beacon, Bamburgh and Creswell which correctly identified the strength as a single aircraft. The aircraft was designated 'Raid 42' and Felicity Ashbee 'told' it to the coast, from where the radar duties were taken over by a network of posts manned by the Royal Observer Corps.[10]

The night of 10/11 May 1941 was very busy for Fighter Command and the British defences, for German bombers were making one of the heaviest attacks of the war on London. Among the buildings seriously damaged was the House of Commons, the interior being gutted and the roof destroyed by incendiary bombs. This was a bad omen for Hess's mission. However, the worst of the Blitz was over for Londoners, since the Luftwaffe began withdrawing to the forthcoming Russian Front. It was several days before Felicity Ashbee realized that she had 'told' Hess on his approach to Northumberland.

A few minutes after the first radar contact was made with Hess's aircraft, orders to attack the intruder were received by No. 13 (Fighter) Group's headquarters at Ouston, near Newcastle-upon-Tyne. In turn, orders were passed to the Duty Controller of the Ouston Sector, one of the three which made up this Group, but only one squadron was in a position to make an interception in this thinly defended area. This was 72 Squadron, based at Acklington in Northumberland, which was equipped with Spitfire IIs.[11] Two Spitfires already on patrol over the Farne Islands were vectored on to the enemy, but Hess's manoeuvres caused confusion and the operators ended up by vectoring these two Spitfires on to their own tracks. (Spitfires were not fitted with airborne interception radar and the pilots were wholly dependent on R/T vectoring by ground control until they came within visual range.)

At 22.20 hours another Spitfire was scrambled from Acklington.[12] This was a Spitfire IIa, serial P8042, flown by Sgt Maurice A. Pocock, an experienced pilot who had fought in the Battle of Britain.[13] Pocock, who ended the war as a flight lieutenant, has a clear recollection of the event. He climbed to 15,000 feet, the altitude originally reported for the enemy aircraft, but saw nothing. Then he turned inland but could see no aircraft beneath against the dark hills of Northumberland. Disappointed at not adding to his tally of victories, he returned to base 35 minutes after take-off.[14]

Meanwhile Hess was successfully avoiding these Spitfires, although he did not see them. On approaching the coast shortly after sunset, he spotted the peak of the Cheviot, 2,676 feet high, in the distance. In his letter to 'Buz', he described the coastline as a 'heavenly, polar-like view'.[15] Certainly, his navigation had been astonishingly accurate after three hours over the sea without a visual pinpoint. In this early twilight, he could see two British destroyers sailing at an oblique angle across his track near Holy Island, slightly to the north-west of Bamburgh, as well as a number of small boats. An alteration of course was made towards the Cheviot, to avoid any anti-aircraft fire. He also noticed that mist was obscuring the English coast. Although this was not thick, the moon had risen and was shining on the top of this layer, making visibility more difficult from above and offering some protection from RAF fighters. He pushed the control column forward and went into a shallow dive from 5,000 metres, increasing speed and streaking down to very low level. This must have been the action which kept him out of sight of the two patrolling Spitfires and the one flown by Maurice Pocock. Hess wrote in his letter, 'It seems that there had been a Spitfire some 5 km behind me.'[16]

At 22.23 hours his aircraft was reported by sound and bearing from the Royal Observer Corps (ROC) A.2 post at Embleton, just inland from the coast about 24 km south-east of Holy Island.[17] This network of small posts had been constructed before the war and covered the entire country, with various regional headquarters. The posts were manned by about 10,000 civilian volunteers, many of whom had served in the First World War and were beyond military age, and others who were still too young to join the armed forces. The ROC had been mobilized under the RAF's Fighter Command. The equipment in each post consisted of no more than a simple theodolite, binoculars and a telephone, but the contribution made by this body of men had proved so effective during the Battle of Britain that King George VI had conferred the title of 'Royal' on the Corps. On 10 May 1941 the progress of the intruding aircraft across England and Scotland was accurately reported to Fighter Command by the ROC until the moment it crashed.

A.2 post came under the control of No. 30 (ROC) Group, which operated from Durham post office. Two minutes after the first report, another came in from the head observer of A.3 post at Chatton in Northumberland, George W. Green. This was the first correct identification of the type of aircraft, for Green recognized the silhouette in the twilight as an 'Me110 at 50 feet'. Me110 was the British designation for the Messerschmitt Bf110. No. 30 (ROC) Group passed this information immediately to No. 13 (Fighter) Group, but the controller thought that they must be mistaken and that the aircraft was a Dornier Do17 bomber. There seemed no logical reason why a Bf110 fighter should be flying at that altitude over the countryside. It was assumed that Raid 42 had split and the single aircraft was redesignated 'Raid 42J'.[18]

By now Hess was in his element as an audacious and skilful pilot. He climbed up the side of the Cheviot Hills and slid down the other side into Scotland. Then he turned on to 280 degrees, heading for St Mary's Loch near Broad Law in the southern uplands. People could still be seen in the fields, and he waved cheerfully to them from treetop level. All the time his aircraft was faithfully tracked by a string of ROC posts which continued to report it as an Me110. The speed was recorded as over 300 mph, indicating that he was burning up his remaining fuel at an enormous rate. He made minor alterations of course and at about 22.45 hours passed very close to Dungavel House, about 16 miles south-south-east from the centre of Glasgow.

There was a very small and sloping grass airfield at Dungavel House, privately owned but unused since the beginning of the war. When in use, it had been suitable for light biplanes or some high-wing monoplanes but it was certainly inadequate for a heavy aircraft such as the Messerschmitt Bf110. It is not clear whether Hess intended to attempt a crash-landing there or bale out over the sea. In any event he failed to recognize either Dungavel House or the little airfield in the late twilight and decided to climb and continue to the west coast, where he could check his position.

At 22.34 hours, some 9 minutes before passing

Dungavel House, Hess had entered the Ayr Sector of No. 13 (Fighter) Group, which had its headquarters at Homemount, near the village of Monkton, beside Prestwick airfield. This was served by No. 31 (ROC) Group with its headquarters at Galashiels. The duty controller at Monkton on the night of 10/11 May 1941 was Squadron Leader C. Hector Maclean, a pilot who had been seriously wounded on 26 August 1940 during the Battle of Britain. Flying Spitfire I serial X4187 of 602 Squadron from Westhampnett in Sussex, he had been hit in the leg during a combat over Selsey Bill with a Bf109E-4 flown by *Leutnant* Zeis of 1/Jagdgeschwader 53. In considerable agony, he had flown back to Westhampnett and made a belly landing, but lost a foot from his injuries. After a lengthy spell in hospital followed by convalescence, he had returned to the RAF for ground duties.

When Galashiels reported the presence of an Me110 intruding into his area, Maclean's heart sank, for he thought the information must be incorrect and, in his own words, that he was facing a 'cock-up'. As with the other duty controllers, he knew that such an aircraft did not normally carry enough fuel to make a return flight. He asked the ROC to check with its observers, but nevertheless ordered a nightfighter into the air.[19]

One minute later, at 22.35 hours, Plt Off William A. Cuddie of 141 Squadron based at Ayr took off in Boulton Paul Defiant serial T4040, with Sgt Hodge in the turret, to intercept the 'hostile' aircraft.[20] Several of these two-seater Defiants were employed as nightfighters after their disastrous encounters with Messerschmitt Bf109s in the daylight operations during the Battle of Britain. Although they were only a temporary expedient while squadrons were awaiting the arrival of Beaufighters fitted with airborne interception radar, Defiants were proving quite successful in their new role, even though they were not fitted with radar. They operated by flying below their targets and looking upwards for enemy bombers silhouetted against the night sky. The four Browning .303 inch machine-guns in the turret made short work of any aircraft unfortunate enough to receive a full blast in its belly. During the course of the week, 141 Squadron had already accounted for three Heinkel He111s on the Monday, three more on the Tuesday, and yet another as well as a Junkers Ju88 on the Wednesday. Most of these bombers had crashed overland and had been confirmed. This was probably the most dangerous period for Hess in his entire flight, for he was extremely vulnerable while no longer at treetop level. Arriving over the west coast at 22.55 hours, he saw what he termed 'a fairy-like view', with 'steep mountainous islands visible in the moonlight and fading twilight'.[21] This must have been one of the Cumbrae islands, for his reported track passed very close to these prominent landmarks.

Hess then turned back inland, following a zigzag path and trying to use the railway line to Kilmarnock to lead him towards Dungavel, but the ground below was too dark. All the time, Cuddie was pursuing him.[22] Hess later told the Duke of Hamilton that he had seen this nightfighter, but thought it was a Hurricane. By now, fuel was getting very low and he decided it was time to bale out. He climbed to about 6,000 ft, switched off the engines and feathered the propellers, although the starboard engine continued to fire until he throttled it right back. He opened the non-jettisonable cockpit roof, which was hinged back against the antenna mast and held in place by the slipstream. He also unfastened the two side windows, which then hung against the side of the fuselage at an angle of about 20 degrees. Only the gunner/navigator's canopy section could be jettisoned, from handles in this compartment which Hess could not reach. By now, it was about 23.06 hours, more than five hours since he had left Augsburg.

Hess tried to clamber out of the cockpit but the machine

was still flying too fast and the slipstream forced him back again, to his surprise and dismay. He was now in great danger, for the aircraft was sinking rapidly towards the ground. Then he suddenly remembered that one baled out of a modern aircraft by turning it on its back. In a rather panicky move, he pulled back on the stick to try a half-loop instead of a half-roll, but the centrifugal force drained the blood from his head and he blacked out. Luck was on his side, for when he came to the machine was standing on its tail, almost stalling. He pushed vigorously with his legs and fell backwards into the air. As he did so, the machine finally stalled and he saw it plunging earthwards beneath him.[23] He pulled on the D-ring of his ripcord and his parachute opened, while the Messerschmitt crashed and burst into flames at 23.09 hours.[24] A few seconds later he hit the ground hard and was dragged forward by his parachute. For the second time he lost consciousness.

# CHAPTER FIVE

# *The Next Ten Days*

The first reaction to Hess's arrival in Scotland is best described in his own words, in the letter he wrote to his son in June:

> I woke up in a German-looking meadow, not realizing where I was and what was happening to me. When I first saw my parachute lying behind me, it became clear to me that I had arrived in Scotland, the first landing place of my 'Plan'. I was lying some ten metres from the front door of a house of a Scottish goatherd. People came running towards me, alarmed by the burning aircraft. They looked at me in a compassionate way.[1]

The place where he had landed was Floors Farm to the west of Eaglesham in Renfrewshire, 12 miles to the west of his intended destination of Dungavel House.[2] The 'house' was in fact a cottage occupied by David McLean, who was not a goatherd but a head ploughman. He was a bachelor of about forty-five years of age, and lived there with his mother. He was preparing to go to bed when he heard the noise of an aircraft overhead. Then the engines stopped and a few minutes later there was an explosion. Looking out of the window, he saw a parachute floating down and went outside to investigate. The man beneath hit the ground and was dragged along by the billowing parachute. McLean helped him to his feet and saw that he was wearing a foreign uniform underneath his flying clothes. When asked if he was German, Hess replied in good

English, 'Yes, I am Hauptmann Alfred Horn. I have an important message for the Duke of Hamilton.' (The reason for his use of this alias is not clear, but it is worth pointing out that Alfred was the name of Hess's brother, Horn the name of his wife's stepfather Carl Horn, and the initials A.H. were also those of Adolf Hitler.)

William Craig, sixty-eight years old, came out of a nearby farmhouse and went off to report the incident and get help.[3] Hess had been injured slightly, in the back and the right ankle. He attributed the latter injury to catching his foot in his parachute harness when he jumped,[4] but it is more likely that it was the result of the more common accident of hitting the tail as the aircraft plunged downwards.

McLean checked the German for weapons and then gathered up the parachute. He was much smaller than Hess but helped him into the cottage, where his mother was busy dealing with the excitement in the usual British manner by making a pot of tea. Hess refused tea but asked for a glass of water. His hosts were impressed by his courteous manner, well-cut uniform, hand-made flying boots, and gold wristwatch.[5]

News of the parachutist spread fast. Within two minutes of his arrival, Giffnock police station telephoned the headquarters of the 3rd Battalion, Renfrewshire Home Guard, at Clarkston. In turn, this unit telephoned its outpost at Picket Law, not far from Floors Farm. As it happened, the Messerschmitt had also been spotted by two Home Guard officers en route to inspect this outpost. They had seen the pilot leave the aircraft and the subsequent crash, indicating that Hess was very low when he baled out. These two officers and two of the outpost guard rushed towards Floors Farm and met yet another Home Guard officer who lived nearby and was driving to the scene, together with two Royal Artillery soldiers he had gathered from an Army camp on Bonnyton Moor.

The two parties decided to converge on Floors Farm by separate routes.[6]

The officer with the two gunners arrived first. According to Hess, this officer was in civilian clothes, had been drinking heavily and prodded him continually in the back with his revolver in order to march him off to a police station. Then another officer suggested they should go elsewhere, but the first officer protested and jabbed Hess in the stomach with his revolver. However, they decided between them to go to 'another house', where one of the 'Tommies' gave Hess a very welcome bottle of milk.[7]

In fact, Hess was taken by car to the Home Guard headquarters at Busby, near Glasgow, and arrived there at 00.14 hours on 11 May. It was wondered if he should be locked up in a cell in Giffnock police station, but after some telephone discussions relating to his evident importance, injuries and increasing tiredness, it was decided that he should be held in Maryhill Barracks in Glasgow. While waiting for an escort from the 11th Cameronians (Scottish Rifles), various visitors arrived. Two police detectives helped to search Hess for drugs, arms and papers. His possessions were taken off him and listed. A German-speaking clerk from the Polish Consulate in Glasgow, Roman Battaglia, arrived to help as an interpreter.[8] Then the Scottish Area Commandant of the ROC, Major Graham Donald, arrived, together with an RAF officer. They had already driven out to examine the wreckage of the German aircraft and verified that it was a 'stripped Me110', brand new and out of fuel.[9]

Hess told Donald that he had arrived deliberately and had a vital secret message for the Duke of Hamilton. He said that he had started from Munich and agreed that he did not have enough fuel to get back. Donald studied his face and thought that he must be Rudolf Hess, although the prisoner insisted he was Alfred Horn. In his report, Donald noted 'he is, if one may apply the term to a Nazi, quite a gentleman . . . I found him to be a very interesting and quite pleasant fellow, not in the least of the tough young Nazi type, but definitely an officer who might be a very important man in higher Nazi circles.'[10] Soon after this interview, the prisoner was taken to Maryhill Barracks and placed under armed guard in the sick bay, where his injuries could receive medical attention.

So far Hess's flight had been accomplished with quite remarkable accuracy, but now the flaws in his prior intelligence began to show up. Perhaps he hoped that he would simply be able to knock on the door of Dungavel House and be ushered into the duke's presence by the butler. However, even if his navigation had been crowned by such success, he would have found that his potential host was not at home, for Wing Commander the Duke of Hamilton and Brandon was one of four brothers who were active serving officers in the RAF. Before the war he had been on the staff of the Directorate of Flying Training but on 30 July 1940 had taken over command of RAF Turnhouse, a fighter station near Edinburgh, having arrived there twelve days earlier.[11]

Turnhouse was the third Sector Headquarters of No. 13 (Fighter) Group, the other two being Ouston to the south and Ayr to the west, and the Duke of Hamilton had had little sleep for three nights. Among other matters, he had watched the progress of Hess's Messerschmitt on the plotting board and had assumed that three Hurricanes in the air from Ousten were among those sent up to intercept it. These were, however, aircraft of the recently formed 317 (Polish) Squadron and the pilots were still under training, learning RAF flying procedures in English and practising night flying. They were not vectored on to the intruder.[12] Hamilton had also watched the Defiant from Ayr closing with the enemy and had been disappointed at the failure to shoot it down. After this, he had gone to bed, feeling extremely tired.[13]

Soon afterwards, he was aroused from his sleep and told to take an urgent telephone call from the duty controller in the Ayr sector, Squadron Leader C. Hector MacLean, who had been alerted by the police. The two men were old friends, for MacLean had served in 602 Squadron during part of the time when the Marquis of Clydesdale (as the Duke of Hamilton was then) had been in command. According to MacLean the conversation went as follows:

'What's all this about, Hector?'

'A German captain has parachuted from an Me110 and wants to see you.'

'Good heavens, what does he want to see me about?'

'I don't know, he won't say.'

'What do you think I should do about it?'

'I think you should go and see him.'

'Yes, I think I will.'[14]

MacLean told his Operations Room that the Duke of Hamilton would see the prisoner, but this interview did not take place until 10.00 hours on 11 May, when Hamilton and an intelligence officer arrived at Maryhill Barracks by car from Turnhouse, after a few hour's sleep. Hamilton could find nothing in *King's Regulations* to cover such an incident, but thought he should take MacLean's advice.[15] They first examined Hess's effects, which included a Leica camera, photographs of himself and his son, medicines and the visiting cards of Karl and Albrecht Haushofer. The prisoner asked if he could speak to Hamilton alone and his request was granted.

Hess introduced himself by his correct name and said that he had seen Hamilton at the Olympic Games of 1936 in Berlin. He had come on a mission of humanity, for Hitler did not want to defeat Britain but instead hoped to stop the fighting. He had tried to arrange a meeting with Hamilton in Lisbon, via Albrecht Haushofer, and also made three previous attempts to reach Britain. He thought that Hamilton would understand his point of view and suggested that he should 'get together with members of his party to talk things over with a view of making peace proposals'. Meanwhile, he wanted Hamilton to approach the king for his 'parole', since he had come unarmed and of his own free will.[16]

The discussion was mainly conducted in English, which Hess spoke quite well, although he had difficulty understanding Hamilton, who had almost no knowledge of German. It was clear, however, that Hess had very little comprehension of the British political system of government. He did not seem to realize that a coalition government had been formed on the outbreak of war or that Hamilton had been in the same political party as Winston Churchill in the period when he had been a Member of Parliament. Above all, he had completely misjudged the man in believing that he would take any action that would hinder Britain's successful prosecution of the war. Hamilton told Hess that if Britain made peace now, the two countries would be back at war within two years. However, he believed that the prisoner was genuinely Hess and suggested that he should return with an interpreter.

After this astonishing encounter, Hamilton and his intelligence officer drove out to Eaglesham to inspect the Messerschmitt, and removed certain instruments. Then they went back to Turnhouse, where Hamilton reported to the Air Officer Commanding No. 13 (Fighter) Group, Air Vice-Marshal John O. Andrews, and asked for permission to communicate an important matter to the Foreign Office. With official agreement, his next move was to try to telephone the permanent secretary of the Foreign Office, Sir Alexander Cadogan, to ask for an urgent appointment. While he was arguing against bureaucratic obstruction with an official, the prime minister's private secretary, Jock Colville, walked into the room and took over the telephone.

According to Hamilton's report, Colville said: 'The Prime Minister sent me over to the Foreign Office as he is informed that you have some information. I have just arrived and I would like to know what you propose to do.'[17]

By coincidence, Colville had been reading a popular book of the day, *The Flying Visit* by Peter Fleming. This was a fantasy about Hitler parachuting into England to make peace. By further coincidence there was a secret belief that Hitler might be sky-jacked and flown to RAF Lympne in Kent by his private pilot, Hans Bauer, who was reported to be dissatisfied with Germany's conduct of the war. This information had come from the British air attaché in Bulgaria and was so convincing that Air Vice-Marshal Arthur T. Harris, who worked at the Air Ministry before taking over Bomber Command, made arrangements for the reception with Air-Vice Marshal Trafford Leigh-Mallory of No. 11 (Fighter) Group. It was thought that Hitler's personal aircraft, a Focke-Wulf Fw200 Kondor, would approach the airfield with its wheels down. Two platoons of soldiers were stationed at Lympne to act as guards, and other detailed arrangements were made. A date for a possible arrival was given as 25 March 1941, but when the aircraft did not turn up the arrangements were held in place until the end of May, when the plan was abandoned.[18] Colville was probably aware of Goering's proposal to visit England in late August 1939 as well as Germany's peace overtures to Britain after the collapse of France. In his biography he wrote, 'I felt sure that either Hitler or Goering had arrived.'[19] However, he was thinking of the wrong Nazis.

Hamilton asked Colville if he could have a car at RAF Northolt within half an hour. He jumped into a Hurricane of 213 Squadron (which at the time was non-operational at Turnhouse pending posting via the aircraft carrier HMS *Furious* to Malta and then to Western Desert Air Force in Egypt) and flew to Northolt in Middlesex. As soon as he taxied in, an airman told him that he should fly on to RAF Kidlington in Oxfordshire. He switched off the Merlin engine and got out to study a map. While he was doing so, a mechanic began unwisely to prime the engine. As Hamilton wrote, 'It is a peculiarity of this type of engine that, if it were ever primed while hot, it simply would not start again until it had been given time to cool down again.'

Hamilton must have been furious at this delay, and eventually told the duty officer to find another aircraft. A Miles Magister trainer was provided and he flew to Kidlington, landing after dark. A car was waiting for him at the airfield and he was taken to Ditchley Hall, the sixteenth-century baronial mansion of Ronald Tree, the parliamentary private secretary to the Ministry of Information, where Churchill was staying for the weekend. When shown in by a 'very pompous and smart' butler, he felt dishevelled and tired, but was allowed to wash before joining the prime minister and the other guests.

Churchill was in 'tremendous form, cracking jokes' and told him, 'Now, come and tell us this funny story of yours'. However, dinner was served first and Hamilton later talked to him in company with the Secretary of State for Air, Sir Archibald Sinclair. The discussion was quite brief but Churchill looked at some of Hess's photographs and was 'somewhat taken aback' at the news. However, he insisted on breaking off so that he could watch a Marx Brothers film which was about to be shown, entitled *Go West*. Hamilton fell asleep during the showing, but more details of Hess's arrival were discussed afterwards and he stayed in Ditchley Hall overnight.

The following morning Hamilton accompanied Churchill to 10 Downing Street, where the matter was discussed with members of the War Cabinet and Chiefs-of-Staff. It was decided to make a positive identification of the prisoner with the help of an expert on German affairs,

Sir Ivone Kirkpatrick, who had met Hess on several occasions when he was First Secretary to the British Embassy in Berlin before the war. A de Havilland Rapide was found to take the two men to Turnhouse, refuelling en route at the fighter airfield at RAF Catterick in Yorkshire.

Up to this time the British had made no announcement of Hess's arrival while in Germany there was considerable consternation and uncertainty. According to Helmut Kaden, Hess's party waited at Haunstetten for four hours after his take-off before Pintsch pulled an envelope from his pocket and said, 'Now I have an unpleasant mission. I have to go to the Obersalzberg.' On the following day, however, flying went on as usual and nobody at Augsburg-Haunstetten airfield gave much thought as to where Hess might have landed his Messerschmitt Bf110 radio code VJ+OQ.[20]

It seems likely that the first to incur the wrath of the Nazi hierarchy was Willy Messerschmitt. At 22.00 hours on the evening of Hess's departure, he was telephoned by Goering, who demanded an urgent interview. It may be argued that Goering would have told Hitler of Hess's flight by this time, but bearers of bad news are seldom popular, especially in a dictatorship, and the Führer was not noted for any compassion towards those who incurred his displeasure. Goering's interview with Messerschmitt took place the following morning, according to an account published in the *Frankfurter Neue Presse* of May 1947. Goering pointed his baton at Messerschmitt and shouted: 'I suppose anyone can come and fly one of your machines!'

'Hess was not anyone, but the *Stellvertreter*,' replied Messerschmitt.

'You should have known that the man was crazy!' Goering shouted.

'How could I have known that anyone so high in the

Third Reich was crazy?' Messerschmitt responded. 'If that were the case, you should have procured his resignation!'

Goering roared with laughter, told Messerschmitt to carry on manufacturing aircraft, and promised to shield him from the wrath of Hitler. The content of this interview also corresponds with another given by Messerschmitt to a team from the US Bombing Survey in Germany after the war. Messerschmitt was not arrested and it appears that none of those who worked at Haunstetten fell foul of the Gestapo.

Hess's relatives and friends, and those in his entourage, were very unlucky. On the morning of 11 May Hitler was told that someone wanted to see him urgently. He responded angrily by saying that he was reading military reports and could not be disturbed. However, when told that Hess's adjutant Karlheinz Pintsch had been ordered to deliver an important message for him, he allowed the interview. The exact content of Hess's letter to Hitler has been lost, but Ilse Hess had a copy at one time and remembered that it began, 'My Führer, when you receive this letter I shall be in England.' Hitler's reaction was described by his architect Albert Speer, who happened to be waiting with some drawings. In his autobiography, he wrote:

> While I was leafing through my sketches once more, I suddenly heard an inarticulate, almost animal-like outcry. Then Hitler roared, 'Bormann at once! Where is Bormann?' Bormann was told to get in touch with Goering, Ribbentrop, Goebbels and Himmler by the fastest possible means.[21]

The outcome was predictable. Pintsch and Hess's other adjutant Alfred Leitgen were arrested, as well as all close members of his entourage. Albrecht Haushofer was rounded up, as was Hess's brother Alfred, although Ilse was left in peace after questioning. Hess's letter also recommended that a statement be issued stating that he was mad, provided his peace mission proved unsuccessful. With no word from Britain and no knowledge of his deputy's fate, Hitler authorized an announcement that was broadcast by the Nazi Party at 20.00 hours the following day, 12 May:

> Party Member Hess, who has been expressly forbidden by the Führer to use an aircraft because of a disease which has been becoming worse for years was, in contradiction of this order, able to get hold of an aircraft recently. Hess again took off on Saturday, 10 May, at about 18.00 hours from Augsburg on a flight from which he has not yet returned. A letter he left behind unfortunately showed traces of mental disturbances which justify the fear that Hess was the victim of hallucinations. The Führer at once ordered the arrest of Hess's adjutants, who alone knew of this flight and who in contradiction of the Führer's ban, of which they were aware, did not prevent the flight or report it at once. The National Socialist Movement has, unfortunately in these circumstances, to assume that Party Comrade Hess has crashed or met with a similar accident.[22]

Hamilton and Kirkpatrick were told of this German broadcast shortly after they landed at Turnhouse. At 15.30 hours on the previous day, Hess had been taken to Buchanan Castle, a military hospital at Drymen near Loch Lomond, and the two men drove to this location. They arrived after midnight and found that Hess was asleep. He was woken up and, after having been positively identified by Kirkpatrick, went into a long harangue about the iniquities heaped upon Germany by Britain, and set out his peace terms. The main burden of these was that Britain should give Germany a free hand in Europe, while Germany would allow Britain a free hand in her Empire, apart from returning the colonies which had been confiscated from the Fatherland after the First World War.[23] The two men found this dissertation very tedious and were glad to terminate the interview in the early morning.

Rumours of Hess's arrival had been circulating for several hours, and the BBC and the press were allowed to release the information. The reports of Hess's safety in custody reached Germany immediately, to the consternation of Hitler but giving Ilse Hess the intense relief of knowing that her husband was alive. On 13 May, Hitler's 'Minister of Propaganda and Popular Enlightenment', Dr Paul Josef Goebbels, recorded in his diary:

> I receive a telephone call from the Berghof. The Führer is quite shattered. What a sight for the world's eyes: the Führer's deputy a mentally disturbed man. Dreadful and unthinkable. Now we shall have to grit our teeth.[24]

Goebbels instructed the press and radio to report the matter without comment, and of course the German broadcast was picked up immediately in Britain:

> On the basis of a preliminary examination of the papers which Hess left behind him, it would appear that Hess was suffering from the hallucination that by undertaking a personal step in connection with the Englishmen with whom he was formerly acquainted it might be possible to bring about an understanding between Germany and Britain. As has since been reported from London, Hess parachuted from his plane near the place in Scotland which he selected as his destination and was found there, apparently in an injured condition.[25]

This statement was inaccurate, since the principal 'Englishman' Hess wished to meet was the Duke of

Hamilton, whom he had never met, and his injuries proved to be fairly minor. Also on 13 May two reports about Hess's medical condition were submitted to the Officer Commanding the Military Hospital at Drymen, Colonel R.A. Lennie, from members of his staff.[26] One came from Major A. Dorset Harper, a surgical specialist. He stated that X-rays showed the patient had sustained a chip fracture of the 12th thoracic vertebra and a small fragment of bone detached from the lower end of the right tibia. There was also extensive bruising on the inner side of the ankle region. The other report came from Lieutenant-Colonel J. Gibson Graham, who was in charge of the Medical Division. He stated that temperature, pulse and respiration were within normal limits and that the patient did not seem ill, apart from the minor injuries he had received and a somewhat confused head after the recent strains he had undergone. An X-ray of the chest showed that the lungs were clear, apart from a small calcified area in the right upper zone.[27]

It is interesting to note that this 'calcified area' seems to tally with a report dated 2 June 1941 received by MI5 from the Defence Security Office in Egypt, which included the statement 'I know for a fact that Rudolf used to suffer from tuberculosis as this was told to me by his mother'.[28]

Both medical specialists confirmed that Hess could be removed safely. Two days later Colonel Lennie reported to the Headquarters of Scottish Command in Edinburgh.[29] He stated that the prisoner seemed to have no history of organic disease but complained of vague abdominal pains and sleeplessness caused by changing of the guard. Hess was also very indignant because his drugs had been taken from him. He requested four books, Jerome's *Three Men in a Boat*, Grenfell's *Sea Power*, Liddell Hart's *Dynamic Defence*, and one about Scotland. Lennie sent another report on the following day, 16 May. This stated that no evidence of problems with the gall bladder, intestinal tract and abdomen could be discovered by X-rays. However, the prisoner was a 'definite health neurotic' who was prepared to talk endlessly on this subject and had relied on homeopathic doctors, qualified and unqualified. He had insisted on having his buttocks swabbed down with an antiseptic lotion after rising from the X-ray couch, to preclude any possibility of infection.

The medical officers at Drymen saw the last of their strange patient on the day of this report, for Hess was taken by night train from Glasgow to London and from there to the Tower of London, where he arrived at about 10.30 hours on the next day, 17 May. His stay in this historic location was quite short, for he was removed on 21 May to Mytchett Place in Surrey, a secure unit that had been chosen as suitable for a prisoner of his status.[30]

# CHAPTER SIX

## Hess's Messerschmitt

It has always been recognized that the machine in which Hess flew to Scotland was a Messerschmitt Bf110. However, many aircraft in both the Luftwaffe and the RAF underwent modifications during their periods of service, usually to incorporate improvements in performance or to adapt the machine for various specialized duties. While it may seem unnecessarily pedantic to identify the precise variant of Bf110 flown by Hess, it does have some importance in demonstrating to readers, including air historians, that the machine was capable of flying from Augsburg to the area of Glasgow but that it could not make a return flight to Germany or to German-occupied territory.

The remains of Hess's machine were collected on 11 May 1941, the day after the crash, by No. 63 Maintenance Unit at Carluke, near Glasgow.[1] It was identified as Messerschmitt Bf110 works number 3869 and was found to have four machine-guns in the nose, still packed with grease, but no ammunition. The wreckage was at first stored in a dump, together with the remains of numerous other aircraft which had crashed in Scotland, but responsibility for salvage and disposal of crashed enemy aircraft rested with the Ministry of Aircraft Production. The pieces of the aircraft were hastily gathered up from the dump and collected on 16 May by Flight Lieutenant Frank E. Cowlrick of No. 43 (Maintenance) Group, based at Andover in Hampshire. Loaded on an RAF 'Queen Mary' articulated low-loader and labelled for the benefit of interested bystanders, the wreckage was transported down to Oxford and placed in storage. On 22 May J. Eaton Griffith of the Ministry of Aircraft Production wrote to the prime minister's office, asking for Churchill's views on the future of the machine. A reply was sent three days later, stating that it should not be used for propaganda and recommending that he should 'hold on to it for the present'.[2]

Public interest in the matter of Hess's arrival waned when so many dramatic events occurred in the course of the war, but after the Allied victory the wreckage was released for exhibition purposes. Nowadays the only remains are the two engines and part of the fuselage aft of the cockpit, but without the tail unit. One of the engines is in the possession of the Royal Air Force Museum in Hendon while the other engine and the fuselage, clearly showing the radio code VJ+OQ on the port side, are on exhibition at the Imperial War Museum in London. For many years the Imperial War Museum has labelled the engine as a Daimler-Benz 601A giving a maximum power of 1,100 hp at 12,140 ft, and the fuselage as part of a Messerschmitt Bf110. From this labelling, it has been assumed by some researchers that the machine was probably a Bf110D-2, a long-range fighter-bomber which was powered by these engines, could be fitted with the large 900-litre drop-tanks, and was in service at the time Hess made his flight.

The Imperial War Museum is a highly respected institution which is widely admired throughout the world for the excellence of its exhibits as well as for its well-informed staff. The authors of this book are among its devotees, but they felt obliged to point out in an article published in 1995 that this labelling was not correct.[3]

The first clue can be seen in the engine at the Royal Air Force Museum. This carries the letter 'N' painted in white on the top. The engine at the Imperial War Museum is mounted upside down but a staff member has agreed in writing that it also carries the letter 'N' on its top.[4] This letter can also be seen in old photographs of the wreckage while being transported or on display. This means that the engine is not a DB601A of 1,100 hp, which used 87-octane fuel, but a DB601N of 1,175–1,200 hp, which used 100-octane fuel. The letter 'N' was painted on the side of the engine cowlings as well as on the engines themselves, to ensure that the ground mechanics filled the fuel tanks with the correct petrol. In external appearance the two engines were identical, but the 100-octane fuel gave the DB601N engine a higher compression ratio and greater efficiency than the DB601A fitted in other aircraft.

However, the identification of the correct type of engine does not in itself establish the aircraft variant, for seven versions of the Bf110 fitted with the DB601N engine were in service at the time Hess made his flight. These were the Bf110C-4B/N fighter-bomber, the Bf110C-5/N photo-reconnaissance aircraft, the Bf110C-7/N fighter-bomber, the Bf110D-2/N long-range fighter-bomber, the Bf110D-3/N long-range escort, the Bf110E-1/N heavy fighter-bomber and the Bf110E-2/N long-range fighter-bomber. Fortunately there is other evidence which enables the detective work to continue.

It can be seen on the fuselage on display at the Imperial War Museum that there is a groove running along the top of the port side. This groove carried a cable which enabled the second crew member to release an inflatable rubber dinghy in the event of a ditching in the sea. The end of the cable itself, as well as the groove, can also be seen in one of the photographs taken on the site where it crashed. But this method of releasing the dinghy was employed only in Bf110s with extended tail sections.[5] Of the seven variants listed above, only the Bf110D-3/N and the Bf110E-2/N were built with this extended tail and also fitted with the DB601N engines.[6] In addition, both could carry the 900-litre drop-tanks, which were made partly of plywood and partly of metal at this time, although wholly metal drop-tanks were introduced later.

With the possibility of the variant whittled down to only two, more evidence has to be uncovered. In another photograph of the wreckage, a rectangular opening on the starboard side of the fuselage can be seen. This is a vent near frame eight which could be opened to provide fresh air for the heater in the position of the second crew member.[7] But this vent was fitted only in the Bf110E variants and those which followed later. Thus the only remaining possibility for Hess's machine is the Bf110E-2/N long-range fighter-bomber.

There is another piece of evidence to confirm this conclusion. In one of the photographs of the wreckage, four parallel lines can be seen near the leading edge of the undersurface of the starboard wing, near the fuel pipes for the 900-litre drop-tanks. It has proved possible to establish that these mark out the attachment points for ETC50 bomb racks, a version of the *Elektrische Trägervorrichtung für Cylinderbomben* (electrically operated carrier for cylindrical bombs) which were standardized on some of the Bf110E variants.

The chief test pilot at the Messerschmitt Works, Helmut Kaden, was unfailingly courteous and informative in his letters to the authors of this book before his death on 26 February 1992 at the age of eighty-one. He expressed the opinion that Hess's machine was probably a Bf110E-1/N, a near-relative of the Bf110E-2/N. But this recollection cannot be correct, since the Bf110E-1/N did not have an extended rear fuselage and also it was fitted with 300-litre drop-tanks. It is possible that Hess's machine began life as a Bf110E-1/N, but alterations in production frequently took place at the Messerschmitt Works. There are numerous examples of works numbers originally allocated to one variant being switched to another, until the system was regularized in 1943. An example can be seen in the records of Messerschmitt production batches available at the National Archives in Washington D.C. On 3 July 1940 a batch of Bf110D-0s were built, of which six were changed into Bf110D-1s and fifteen into Bf110D-0Bs; some of the individual aircraft works numbers were recorded on document *Soll-u. 1st – Ablieferung der Flugzeuge* (estimated and actual supply of aircraft) of April 1940.[8] It is possible that Hess asked Willy Messerschmitt for a Bf110E-2/N variant to be included in a production batch of Bf110E-1/Ns, knowing that it possessed attributes that were indispensable to the project he had in mind.

The Messerschmitt Bf110E-2/N was fitted with two 1,200 hp Daimler-Benz engines, twelve-cylinder, inverted-vee and liquid-cooled. For the internal fuel supply, there was a 375-litre main tank in front of the mainspar and a 260-litre reserve tank behind, in each wing between the engines and the fuselage. The machine could also carry two 900-litre drop-tanks, giving a total fuel supply of 3,070 litres. It could achieve a maximum speed of 473 km/hr at sea level or 562 km/hr at 7,000 metres. Its cruising speed at 5,000 metres was 490 km/hr. It could climb to 6,000 metres in 11 minutes and the service ceiling was 10,000 metres. (See Appendix F)

Flying at a cruising speed of 490 km/hr at an altitude of 5,000 metres with the total supply of fuel, the range of the Bf110E-2/N was 2,000 km. The distance in a direct line from Augsburg to Glasgow is about 1,350 km. Of course, Hess did not fly in a straight line or at a constant altitude. He made several diversions and alterations in altitude before reaching the coast of Northumberland. Then he opened up his throttles and burnt up fuel at a furious rate when flying over the hills of the north of England and southern Scotland. But he had ample fuel to make the journey from Augsburg to Dungavel House, near Glasgow. (See Appendix G)

There have been two major misapprehensions regarding the fuel tanks of Hess's Messerschmitt. One of these stems from three facts. The first fact is that some observers said that they saw a fuel tank under the belly of the aircraft when it was in the air. The second fact arises from the knowledge that Major Graham Donald, the Area Commandant of the ROC, 'rolled the main fuel tank clear of the flames' when he examined the wreckage soon after the crash.[9] The third fact arises from an occasion on 15 August 1940 during the Battle of Britain when about sixty-five Heinkel He111 bombers of *Kampfgeschwader 26*, escorted by about thirty Bf110D-1/R1s of *I./ZG76* (the first Group of *Zerstörergeschwader 76*), flew from Stavanger-Sola in Norway to make an attack on north-east England. Each Bf110 was fitted with a single *Dackelbauch* (Dachshund belly) auxiliary tank beneath the fuselage, to enable it to make the return journey to its base. This single tank was large, made of wood and covered with fabric, but it was not jettisonable. It contained four compartments, three of which carried a total of 1,010 litres of petrol and the fourth 80 litres of oil. The contraption was very unwieldy as well as highly explosive, even when empty. It became a well-known and favourite target for RAF fighter pilots, for a single bullet hit could blow a Bf110 to smithereens. Indeed, this is what happened to several of these machines and their unfortunate crews on 15 August 1940. The surviving Bf110s did not return for any other combat during the Battle of Britain.

These three facts have led some authors to believe that the machine which crashed at Floors Farm on 10 May 1940 was fitted with this single belly tank and thus carried insufficient fuel to have flown from Augsburg. It is reasoned that it must have come from Norway, or at least flown a shorter distance than from Augsburg. But this reasoning is incorrect. It is not generally understood that in addition to the two huge drop-tanks under the wings, containing petrol, Hess's Messerschmitt was fitted with a third drop-tank, under the belly. But this tank was small and contained oil, not petrol.

With the failure of the *Dackelbauch* belly tank, another method of increasing the range of the Bf110 had to be found. Thus shackles were fitted under the wings outboard of the engines, with wet-points for the flow of fuel. Drop-tanks of various sizes, containing petrol, could then be carried and were known as *Rüstsatz B2* (Field Conversion Set B2). However, on long flights the machine also used a lot of oil, which was provided in the fourth compartment of the *Dackelbauch* and amounted to 80 litres. Thus another drop-tank was installed, named *Rüstsatz B1*, containing 75 litres of oil. This was positioned underneath the fuselage and could be jettisoned by pulling a lever on the left side of the second crew member's compartment. This must have been the tank which Major Donald rolled away.

Directly behind each engine of the Bf110, there was a tank containing some 35 litres of oil. Each tank had to be replenished every hour of flying time in the Bf110E-2/N with 7.5 litres of oil from the 75-litre drop-tank. The switch-over valve, pumps and jettison handle were situated in the second crew member's compartment. However, it should be noted that in a letter written from Spandau on 12 February 1950, Hess said 'before taking off, I had lived in a world of . . . auxiliary oil pumps'.[10] This indicates that the pumping mechanism was transferred to the pilot's cockpit, which was quite simple technically. Certainly Hess would have been unable to complete his journey without replenishing the oil in the wing tanks. After five hours of flying the *Rüstsatz B1* must have been almost empty, and indeed Major Donald said that it contained 'only three or four gallons of fuel'. On the other hand it would have been extremely difficult, if not impossible, to transfer the jettison handle to the pilot's cockpit, so that the oil tank remained underneath the fuselage until breaking off its shackles when the machine hit the ground.

The other misapprehension concerns the 900-litre drop-tanks. It is sometimes asserted by other authors that one of these tanks was recovered from the Clyde on the day after Hess made his flight. The origin of this report is not given, nor is the precise position from which the tank was recovered. For example, it is not known whether the tank was found in the River Clyde or the Firth of Clyde which extends from the port of Glasgow down the west coast of Scotland for several miles. However, it seems extremely unlikely that a tank could have been dropped into the fairly narrow River Clyde which meanders through the countryside before reaching Clydebank. Although Hess flew over this river, he did not fly over Glasgow and the only real possibility is thus the Firth of Clyde. A detailed examination of the *Admiralty Tidal Stream Atlas* shows that a tank dropped into the area over which Hess flew would have drifted to the coast during the night or the following day.

In any event, whatever tank was recovered could not have come from Hess's aircraft. To explain this statement it is necessary to describe the method of petrol supply in the Messerschmitt Bf110. The engines, both port and starboard, were fed via the self-sealing 375-litre fuel tanks in the wings forward of the spars. In turn these tanks were fed from the drop-tanks, whenever a white warning light showed up on the pilot's instrument panel indicating that a tank was down to 240 litres. The pilot then set a selector lever for the tank-replenishing pump and altered the fuel cock. He switched on the pump and the valve, so that sufficient fuel from the drop-tanks was transferred to the main wing tanks. This procedure was repeated at intervals until the warning lights indicated that the drop-tanks were empty.[11] At this point, the pilot jettisoned the drop-tanks by pulling a handle on the floor beside him. This reduced drag and improved the performance of the Bf110 for the remainder of its flight.

The petrol in Hess's two *Rüstsatz B2* drop-tanks would have been used up around 21.15 hours, three-and-a-half hours after take-off, although there would still have been plenty of oil left in the single *Rüstsatz B1* drop-tank. At this time Hess was still over the North Sea, approaching his 'North Point' before turning to the coast of Northumberland. It is impossible to believe that a pilot of his experience and knowledge would not have jettisoned the two huge drop-tanks when he was nearing the most dangerous part of his flight and needed maximum performance from his aircraft. Moreover, the tanks remained explosive, full of petrol fumes. Every German pilot in that era, no matter how inexperienced and naive, knew such elementary facts. Indeed, Hess could not have gone into his dive, which might have been as fast as 435 mph (700 km/hr), and then achieved his recorded speed of about 300 mph (480 km/hr) with the drag from the two huge tanks. This was the maximum speed of the Bf110E-2/N at extreme low level under optimum flying conditions.

Of course when the fuel in his 375-litre main tanks began to run low, Hess would have replenished them with the contents of the 260-litre reserve tanks in the wings behind the spars. He burnt up almost all this remaining fuel at an enormous rate in the last stages of his journey, but the two drop-tanks had already been jettisoned into the North Sea.

Hess's aircraft was not the only one carrying drop-tanks to fly over Britain in the early part of the war. The first example recorded in a file on this subject in the Public Record Office was reported by the police in Nottingham on 29 August 1940.[12] It was described at first as a 'wooden shaped bomb', but was then found to contain traces of petrol and to be made of plywood built up and glued. Other reports of similar drop-tanks followed from the police in Cambridge, Norfolk, Edinburgh and the Isle of Wight. The Air Ministry was very interested in the smashed remains recovered, for the RAF had not yet developed the use of drop-tanks. A department of Air Intelligence drew up an accurate diagram of a German 'auxiliary petrol tank', which can be seen in this document. There was even a report of a German drop-tank found in North Wales on 12 May 1940, two days after Hess made his flight, although none of a tank recovered from the Clyde.

Drop-tanks of various sizes were in common use by the Luftwaffe at the time, being fitted to other Bf110s as well as aircraft such as Junkers Ju88s engaged on weather reconnaissance and photo-reconnaissance duties. Of course, all major cities and ports such as Glasgow were photographed regularly by such aircraft, and it is probable that any drop-tank recovered from the Clyde came from one of these. We can be certain that it was not dropped from Hess's Messerschmitt.

# CHAPTER SEVEN

# *Prisoner for Life*

Immediately after Hess's capture and positive identification, Winston Churchill had issued an order to the Director of Prisoners of War, Major-General Sir Alan Hunter: 'He should be treated with dignity as if he were an important general who has fallen into our hands.'[1] Thus Hess's imprisonment in the country house of Mytchett Place, near Aldershot in Surrey, was not uncomfortable. He was taken there by ambulance from the Tower of London on 21 May 1940, guarded by two cars containing armed officers. The house and its gardens were designated 'Camp Z' and placed under the command of Colonel A. Malcolm Scott, who ensured that the site was secure and well guarded.

Hess had his own suite of rooms and the company of three young intelligence officers who were quartered in the same building, presumably to relay any information he might let slip in his conversations with them. Meanwhile he was not allowed to read newspapers or listen to the wireless. His requests for another meeting with the Duke of Hamilton were ignored and he became increasingly depressed as it began to dawn on him that his mission was proving a failure. He had already written to the duke on 19 May, during his brief incarceration in the Tower of London. This letter is available in the Public Record Office and a translation from the German demonstrates a state of mental confusion as well as a messianic obsession with the possibility of sacrificing his life in the cause of peace:

My dear Duke,

I feel it necessary that you should know the following facts:

In the letter I left behind for the Führer, I wrote that it was possible that there might be news from England of my death. At the same time some cause of death would be announced – as, for example, suicide or during a dispute. Even if there were reasons to suspect that my death was brought about by elements in England opposed to peace, those in Germany should on no account allow themselves to be influenced thereby to continue the war. It is *only right*, even if my death should have occurred in such strange circumstances, to make peace with those who want peace. This was to be, as it were, my last wish. Probably my death would on the whole be helpful to the whole affair, for only after the conclusion of peace could the English themselves settle accounts with those people who would also probably be responsible for my death. My death would play a great part in this from a propaganda point of view.

I am sure the Führer fully understands this train of thought and would fulfil my wish.

I have, moreover, given my Führer my word that I will not on any account commit suicide. He knows that I will keep my word. So that in any event is ruled out. If opponents of peace try to make trouble, it will certainly be of no avail.

With best wishes,

Rudolf Hess

P.S. Please treat this letter as meant only for you personally and for someone reliable to translate.[2]

There was no reaction from the duke to this letter, for the simple reason that it was never sent to him. He would have been very puzzled if it had arrived, for he had never met Hess prior to his arrival in Scotland and had no sympathy with his cause. This letter appears to be the only one of the many written by Hess during his imprisonment that was prevented from reaching the addressee.

On 28 May 1941 a curious event occurred which cannot be fully explained from the available British or German records. According to a former Army intelligence officer, Lieutenant-Colonel John L. McCowen, this was an attempt by German parachutists to murder Rudolf Hess. There is some evidence in the Public Record Office and elsewhere to support his contention. It begins with a report at 21.55 hours on 27 May, when Lieutenant-Colonel Foss, the commanding officer of 3 Battalion, Bedfordshire Home Guard, was informed by Brigadier D.J.R. Richards, the commanding officer of 49 Anti-Aircraft Brigade, that 'a parachutist agent' would be dropped in the area of Luton on that night 'under cover of bombing'.[3]

It may seem difficult to believe that the British were aware in advance of the arrival of enemy agents, but in fact by this stage of the war it was quite normal. This intelligence was derived from two main sources. The first was via the 'Y' Service, an inter-service organization consisting of numerous wireless stations exclusively devoted to reading foreign W/T and R/T signals. Even before May 1941 the Government Code and Cypher School at Bletchley Park was able to decrypt all the signals sent by the Luftwaffe; this information was relayed to the defence forces when necessary, but without disclosing the source. The second came under what was known as the 'Double Cross System'.[4] This method consisted of 'turning' captured German agents under sentence of death into working for British Intelligence. Some of these agents refused and were executed but several accepted, mostly those who were not German nationals. They used their German W/T sets to send messages to the enemy, giving false information and persuading enemy intelligence that an effective and elaborate spy network was operating in

The luxurious house at Ibrahimieh near Alexandria where the Hess family lived, surrounded by a beautiful garden. It was here that Rudolf Hess spent the first fourteen years of his boyhood. (Source: Wolf Rüdiger Hess)

A studio photograph of Rudolf Hess at the age of seventeen, when attending the Evangelical School in Bad Godesberg. (Source: Wolf Rüdiger Hess)

A studio photograph of *Leutnant der Reserve* (Second Lieutenant of the Reserve) Rudolf Hess taken soon after receiving his commission. (Source: Wolf Rüdiger Hess)

*Leutnant der Reserve* (Second Lieutenant of the Reserve) Rudolf Hess in front of a Fokker Dr.1 Triplane near the Western Front in November 1918. It is not known whether he flew this type of aircraft, which had been withdrawn from front-line service by this time. (Source: Wolf Rüdiger Hess)

Rudolf Hess in the cockpit of a Fokker D.VII of *Jagdstaffel* (Fighter Squadron) 35 at the Western Front. In August 1918 about 800 D.VIIs were in service at the front. (Source: Wolf Rüdiger Hess)

Some members of the *Freikorps Epp*, photographed in May 1919 during a lull in the street battles which were raging in Munich at the time. In the front row on the left, wearing puttees, is *Leutnant der Reserve* Rudolf Hess. (Source: Wolf Rüdiger Hess)

The first aircraft owned by Rudolf Hess was a BFW M23b, serial D-1920, which was donated in July 1931 'for the use of the Party'. He flew the machine during the *Deutschlandflug* (Fly Past) in August of the following year. Powered by an Argus As8 light engine, the two-seater monoplane was similar to the machine in this photograph, serial number D-1856 works number 514; this was registered in June 1930 and owned by *Graf* W.D. du Castell-Rüdenhausen, who lived in Warthe. (Source: Daimler-Benz Aerospace, Unternehmensarchiv)

In August 1931 Rudolf Hess acquired another aircraft, a BFW M23c serial number D-1890. This machine was developed from the M23 and also powered by an Argus As8 engine but the cabin was enclosed and could accommodate two passengers as well as the pilot. The example in this photograph, serial number D-1884 works number 519, was registered in July 1930 and owned by BFW AG. Hess's BFW M23c serial number D-1890 was dismantled in September 1936. (Source: Daimler-Benz Aerospace, Unternehmensarchiv)

In an aircraft of this type, a BFW M35 fitted with a Siemens-Halske SH14a engine, Hess won the first race round the Zugspitze mountain, in 1934. The machine in this photograph was serial D-EQAN, flown by the air acrobatic pilot Willi Stoer, who demonstrated it in many countries during 1935. It had a 'sun-burst' livery while the design bore some early resemblance to the Messerschmitt Bf109 fighter. Some five years later, as the chief test pilot at the Messerschmitt Works at Augsburg, Stoer taught Hess to fly the Messerschmitt Bf110. (Source: Daimler-Benz Aerospace, Unternehmensarchiv)

Rudolf Hess in the cockpit of his BFW M35, receiving congratulations from *Reichsluftsportführer* Bruno Loerzer after wining the annual air race round the Zugspitze mountain on 10 March 1934. The officer between Rudolf Hess and his wife Ilse is Erhard Milch, the former managing director of Lufthansa who later became a field marshal and served as Secretary of State for the Air Ministry. (Source: Roy Conyers Nesbit)

In the second air race flown round the Zugspitze mountain, in 1935, Rudolf Hess and his navigator von Wurmb flew in a BFW M35b two-seater monoplane similar to serial D-2643 in this photograph. It is believed that Hess's machine was powered by the same type of engine as D-2643, a Siemens-Halske Sh14a, but some sources indicate that his aircraft had a smooth engine cowling. On this occasion Hess came sixth in the race. (Source: Daimler-Benz Aerospace, Unternehmensarchiv)

Rudolf Hess photographed at München-Oberwiesenfeld airfield in 1936. The airfield, 4 miles north of Munich, is now the site of the Olympic Stadium. (Source: The late *Flugkapitän a.D.* Helmut Kaden)

This photograph of a Messerschmitt Bf108B-1 *Taifun* (Typhoon), taken in 1937, shows to advantage the graceful lines of this highly successful aircraft. It was powered by an Argus As 10 C-3 engine giving a maximum speed of 303 km/hr, while its endurance was 3 hrs 45 mins. Hess performed a daring flight in a Bf108A, which was fitted with unsatisfactory wing spoilers. After a fatal crash by another pilot, probably resulting from improper use of the spoilers, these were replaced with the more conventional ailerons. (Source: Daimler-Benz Aerospace, Unternehmensarchiv)

Rudolf Hess giving his condolences after the ceremony to the next-of-kin of the sixteen men who were killed in the Nazi uprising of 9 November 1923. Behind him are *Feldmarschall* Wilhelm Keitel and the former *Gauleiter* (District Leader) of Upper Bavaria, Adolf Wagner. (Source: J.L. Roba)

An anniversary of the seizure of power, celebrated at the Sportpalast. Left to right: Führer Adolf Hitler; Reichsminister Josef Goebbels; Deputy Führer Rudolf Hess; Gorlitzer, the Gauleiter of Berlin; Reichsleiter Dr Robert Ley; Reichsminister Hans Lammers. (Source: J.L. Roba)

According to a former member of the Wehrmacht, this photograph of Rudolf Hess in company with German troops was taken on 30 May 1940 near Westende on the Belgian coast. Although this cannot be substantiated by documentary evidence, it is known that Hess visited France and Flanders at this time. Hitler visited Arras, Douai, Bouchain and Cambrai on 2 June 1940 and it is probable that Hess accompanied him. Hess's former unit *Jagdstaffel* 35 was stationed at Bouchain for a while during the First World War and it is highly likely that he visited the airfield. There is also photographic evidence that he visited the fortress of Douaumont, near the place where he received one of his wounds. (Source: Jean Dillen)

Rudolf Hess (on ladder) entering a Messerschmitt Bf110. He flew several machines before selecting the one in which he made his flight to Scotland. On the ground, left to right: Karlheinz Pintsch, *Abteilungsleiter* (Departmental Chief) Piel, Helmut Kaden. On the wing, *Monteur* (Fitter) Griesbauer. (Source: The late *Flugkapitän a.D.* Helmut Kaden)

A Messerschmitt Bf110E, probably photographed at the Messerschmitt Works at Augsburg. The huge drop-tanks, each containing 900 litres of fuel, could be carried by this machine in addition to the fuel in its wing tanks. The photograph does not show whether the machine had an extended fuselage for carrying a dinghy. Thus although the radio code included the letters VJ, one cannot be sure whether it was the Bf110E-2/N radio code VJ+OQ flown by Rudolf Hess to Scotland. (Source: H. Schliephake Archives)

The former chief test pilot for the Messerschmitt Works in Augsburg, *Flugkapitän a.D.* Helmut Kaden, holding a model of a Messerschmitt Bf110. This photograph was taken in 1978, and Helmut Kaden died on 26 February 1992 at the age of eighty-one. (Source: Georges Van Acker)

The main building at Potsdam-Wildpark, as it is at present. In 1936 the participants in the Olympic Games were lodged in this vast complex. During the Second World War it housed such bodies as the *Luftkriegsschule* (School for Air Warfare), the *Generalstab der Luftwaffe* (General Staff of the Air Force), and the *Zentrale Wetterdienst Gruppe* (Central Weather Group) which supplied Hess with weather reports prior to his flight to Scotland. Nowadays the *Korps und Territorialkommando Ost/IV. Korps* (Corps and Territorial Command East/IV. Corps) is billeted here. On 15 July 1992 this complex was renamed the Henning-von-Tresckow-Kaserne building, in memory of the leading member of the unsuccessful Anti-Hitler Resistance, who killed himself with a hand grenade to avoid being forced to betray his comrades to the Gestapo. (Source: Fotoarchiv IV. Korps)

Seven years after they were married, Rudolf and Ilse Hess bought this unobtrusive villa at 48 Harthauser Strasse in the Munich suburb of Harlaching. The Duke and Duchess of Windsor dined with them on the evening of 22 October 1937, after having had tea with Hitler in Berchtesgaden in the afternoon. They had arrived in Berlin on 11 October and had already met several high-ranking Nazis, including Von Ribbentrop and Goering. The purpose of their visit was to pursue the duke's interest in labour relations, although wider issues may have been discussed. On the night of 6/7 September 1943 Munich was attacked by Lancasters and Halifaxes of Bomber Command. The Pathfinders were unable to pick out the target, which was completely covered with cloud, and their markers were not effective. Most of the main force made timed runs from Lake Ammersee and their bombs fell south-west of the town, including the suburb of Harlaching. Hess's villa was completely destroyed. (Source: Wolf Rüdiger Hess)

A rare photograph of Rudolf Hess with his little son Wolf Rüdiger, born on 18 November 1937. Hess adored the boy and gave him the nickname of 'Buz'. (Source: Wolf Rüdiger Hess)

Rudolf Hess in the driver's seat of his private car, either a Mercedes 380 or a 460 Tourenwagen, with his wife Ilse looking on. They seem to be intent on understanding the instrument panel. (Source: Wolf Rüdiger Hess)

A general view of Rudolf Hess's Messerschmitt Bf110, radio code VJ+OQ, after it crashed on Bonnyton Moor, south of Glasgow. (Source: Aeroplane Monthly)

A Scottish captain examining Rudolf Hess's machine after it crashed at Bonnyton Moor. The groove carrying the release cable for the dinghy can be clearly seen along the top of the fuselage, with the cable itself hanging from the rear. At the time Hess made his flight, the extended fuselage carrying the dinghy was a modification made only on variants of the Messerschmitt Bf110D and Bf110E. (Source: Aeroplane Monthly)

In this photograph of the remains of Rudolf Hess's aircraft on an RAF 'Queen Mary' low-loader at Oxford, the letter 'N' can be seen on the engine cover beneath the placard. (Source: After the Battle)

The remains of the fuselage of Hess's Messerschmitt Bf110E-2/N, radio code VJ+OC
works number 3869, showing the groove for the dinghy release cable running
along the top of the fuselage. This photograph was taken in one of the Imperial War
Museum's hangars at Duxford, but the exhibit is now on display at the Imperial
War Museum in Lambeth. (Source: Roy Conyers Nesbit)

This photograph of the underside of the starboard wing of Rudolf Hess's machine
gives clues to the variant of Bf110. Beneath the policeman on the left, near the
leading edge, can be seen the fuel pipes for the 900-litre drop-tank. To the left of
the policeman, near the German cross, can be seen two pairs of parallel slots which
were the attachment points for an ETC50 bomb rack. (Source: Aeroplane Monthly)

Rudolf Hess as a prisoner in December 1945, at Nuremberg Court House awaiting trial. (Source: Aeroplane Monthly)

This distressing photograph of Rudolf Hess in his cell at Spandau, with pictures of the moon behind him, was taken a year before his death on 17 August 1987. When the photograph was taken, he had been incarcerated for over fifty-five years, the majority of this time as a solitary prisoner. This punishment was regarded as completely inhumane by many prominent people throughout the world. (Source: Wolf Rüdiger Hess)

After a temporary burial in a secret location, Rudolf Hess's body was reinterred on 17 March 1988 in the family plot at Wunsiedel in the *Fichtelbirge* (Fichtel Mountains). He now rests between his brother Alfred (1897–1963) and his father Fritz (1864–1941) with his mother Klara (1867–1951). (Source: Wolf Rüdiger Hess)

Reinhard Heydrich standing next to a Messerschmitt Bf109D-1 of *Jagdfliegerschule* (Fighter Training School) 1 at Werneuchen, north-east of Berlin, in late 1939. (Source: J.L. Roba)

Britain. Encouraged by such information, the Germans sent money as well as other agents, to bolster the service.

In response to the warning of an enemy parachute agent, four 40 mm anti-aircraft guns and two searchlights of 73 Light Anti-Aircraft Regiment, 49 Anti-Aircraft Brigade, were deployed at Chalton, about 5 miles north-west of Luton. Aircraft were heard overhead but the records state that these flew too high for the light guns and 'the agent is presumed to have landed safely'.[5] Home Guard patrols were already out and at 03.05 hours one of their reports stated that three bombs had been dropped. It was followed at 03.45 hours by another report: 'Parachute agent believed to have dropped immediately after bombs, is armed and will have parachute marks. Probably making for road Dunstable–London'. Three-quarters of an hour later there was a further report: 'Parachutist believed down one mile east of Sundon [about 6 miles north-west of Luton]. May have travelled some miles or may be lying up. Do not withdraw patrols. Have country searched.' Road blocks were set up, the police were informed, but no arrest was recorded by the Home Guards and their patrols were withdrawn at 08.45 hours.[6]

Another document in the Public Record Office states that four high explosive bombs were dropped at 02.57 hours at Chilton Green viaduct near Hyde, about 3 miles south-east of Luton.[7] One of these fell on Newlands Farm, causing damage to the farmhouse and slightly injuring the occupier.[8] According to an account written after the war by the local newspaper: 'There was a serious night hunt. Home Guards were out. Armed police were out. Some bombs were dropped. They shook up Newlands Farm. Later it was understood that someone was collected not many miles away, but in another county, and never returned to the Fatherland.'[9]

John McCowen was born in County Kerry and served as a gunner in the Territorial Army between the wars. In this period he also spent a year in Hannover and learnt to speak German fluently. In May 1941 he was an acting major in the General Staff, specializing in accumulating information on Admiral Wilhelm Canaris, the head of the *Abwehr* (German military intelligence) and Professor Willy Messerschmitt, the aircraft designer and manufacturer. He was also a friend of Air Vice-Marshal Trafford Leigh-Mallory, the Air Officer Commanding No. 11 (Fighter) Group, who was closely concerned with enemy intelligence and asked him for collaboration in interrogating enemy agents.

McCowen asserts that three of these agents were captured by the SIS (Special Intelligence Service) and that he interrogated them. From 1940 the SIS used Latchmere House at Ham Common in Surrey, known as 'Camp 020', as their interrogation centre. During an interview in 1996 at the age of eighty-nine, McCowen could not recall the names of the German agents but said that they were armed and intent on murdering Hess, in order to prevent him disclosing information about the imminent attack by the Wehrmacht on Russia. They believed that the Deputy Führer was being held in the prisoner-of-war cage at Cockfosters, about 20 miles along the London road from Luton, where Luftwaffe prisoners were normally interrogated after capture. McCowen considered that the men were very brave and thought that they were later executed by firing squad in the Tower of London.[10]

It must be said that these assassins could not have expected to burst into the cage at Cockfosters and gun down Hess in his cell. They would wait outside for a suitable opportunity, advised and assisted by the network of agents they had been led to believe existed in England. Moreover, if three agents were dropped, there must have been more than one aircraft over Luton on that night. A single aircraft was far too cramped to accommodate several agents as well as the crew and the bombs.

At the time, such agents were usually dropped by a small clandestine unit, equipped with Heinkel He111s and Junkers Ju88s, commanded by *Hauptmann* Karl Gartenfeldt, who appears to have been the only operational pilot in the unit in 1941. Under the orders of Major Nicholaus Ritter of the *Abwehr*, he had already ferried some of the *Abwehr*'s spies to England, usually under the cover of a bombing raid by other units. Often taking off from the airfield at Rennes-St-Jacques, his procedure was to fly low over the English Channel in an attempt to keep under the RAF's radar, and then to climb to 20,000 ft. When nearing the dropping zone, he came down lower to drop the agents.[11]

This unit later operated under the orders of the *Reichssicherheithauptamt* or R.S.H.A. (Main Central Security Office). By 20 February 1944 it had expanded considerably and was formed into *Kampfgeschwader 200*. It is known that the *I Gruppe* (which later comprised three *Staffeln*) was commanded by Major Karl Gartenfeldt in March 1944. The records of this unit are almost non-existent, for they were deliberately destroyed by the Germans at the end of the war, while Gartenfeldt himself disappeared and was never traced.[12]

However, there is no record of any men captured after the small raid on Luton, either in police records or elsewhere. Moreover, there is a document in the Public Record Office which lists the burials of all prisoners from 1834 to 1969, when capital punishment was abolished.[13] Although this document records the burials of sixteen enemy agents in the Second World War, there is no evidence of the execution of men who were dropped over Luton on 28 May 1941.

Yet there can be little doubt that something such as described by John McCowen did take place, although it seems probable that the German agents he was asked to interrogate arrived at different times and places. Four such men were arrested and executed in Britain during 1941, one by firing squad in the Tower of London and three by hanging at Wandsworth prison. It is probable that one of the men McCowen interrogated was Karl Richter, a 29-year-old German who parachuted down near London Colney in Hertfordshire on 13 May, in response to fake messages from British Intelligence appealing for money to finance a 'network of agents'. Richter carried money, a compass, a wireless set and a loaded automatic, but was arrested by the police during the following day. It was stated in evidence at his trial that he was believed to be an *Obersturmführer* in the SS. He was a large and powerful man who on the day of his hanging at Wandsworth prison, 10 December 1941, struggled so violently that four warders were required to restrain him.[14] If he was one of the men interrogated by John McCowen, he probably said that he would like to shoot Rudolf Hess as a German traitor. An attempt on Hess's life would have been in accordance with Hitler's comment 'that he deserved to be shot', as recorded in the diaries of Josef Goebbels.[15]

Unaware of these events, Hess continued his imprisonment. He began writing to his family on 3 June, sending almost identical letters to his wife and son and to his parents. In these he merely stated that he was comfortable and living in a house in a beautiful part of England, well guarded by Scots Guards, and that he might not be able to write frequently.[16] However, he was in a dejected frame of mind. This was not improved by an official visit from Lord Simon, the Lord Chancellor, who was given the pseudonym 'Dr Guthrie' for security reasons. He was accompanied by Sir Ivonne Kirkpatrick, code-named 'Dr Mackenzie', while Hess himself was known simply as 'Jonathan'. The purpose of the visit was to try to establish more clearly the reason for Hess's extraordinary flight. The two men arrived at Mytchett Place on 9 June 1941. They spent two-and-a-half hours talking to Hess and Simon submitted a 'Most Secret' report the following day. This included the following comments:

> Hess has come on his own initiative. He has not flown over on the orders or with the permission of Hitler. It is a venture of his own. . . . When he contemplates the failure of his 'Mission', he becomes emotionally dejected. . . . Hess arrived under the impression that the prospects of success of his 'Mission' were much greater than he now realizes. . . . He imagined that there was a strong Peace Party in this country. . . . It is clear to me that Hess's 'plan' is his genuine effort to reproduce Hitler's own mind, as expressed in many conversations. He would never dream of making proposals of his own. He has had in mind the carrying out of his 'self-chosen Mission' ever since the downfall of France, and he 'has always enquired of Hitler what were his conditions of peace, so as to ensure that nothing was changed'. . . . One proof that Hess is merely trying to reproduce what he has heard from Hitler is that Hess breaks down as soon as he is asked for more details. . . . Lastly, I must call attention to Hess's mental condition. . . . He repeated to me his fear that he was being poisoned. He asserted that noises were deliberately made at night to prevent him sleeping. He thought he might be assassinated. When I begged him to behave like a sensible brave man and not give way to such nonsensical ideas, he called attention to his courage in piloting his aeroplane to Scotland. . . . He is certainly hypochondrical and mentally unstable and, to my mind, not at all in a condition when he could keep up a 'bluff' of acting independently when really acting on instructions. There is nothing whatever in his bearing or manner to suggest the cool cold mentality of a clever agent.[17]

The comments from this highly intelligent and perceptive British politician were proved to be precisely correct from subsequent events. It is evident that the visit left Hess in a state of despair, as demonstrated in three letters he wrote a little later. The first was a sycophantic letter to Hitler on 14 June 1941:

My Führer,

My last salute concerns you, for in the last two decades you have fulfilled my life. After the 1918 collapse you made it worth living again. For you and also for Germany, I have been reborn and allowed to start once more. It has scarcely ever been granted to men to serve such a man and his ideas with such success as those subordinate to you. My heartfelt gratitude for all that you have given me and meant to me.

I am writing these lines in the clear knowledge that there is no other way out, however difficult this end may be. I commend my relatives, including my aged parents, to your care. Through you, my Führer, I salute our Greater Germany, which has progressed to an unexpected size. I am dying in the conviction that my last mission, even if it ends in my death, will somehow bear fruit. Maybe my flight will bring, in spite of my death or even through my death, peace and understanding with England.

Heil mein Führer!

Your loyal

Rudolf Hess[18]

He added five lines from Goethe's poem *Das Goettliche* to this letter:

According to eternal, iron, great

Laws

Must we all

Complete the cycles
Of our being.

The second letter was also written on 14 June and addressed to his wife Ilse:

My dear All,

Since I am forced to put an end to my life, all my last greetings and thanks for what you have meant to me. The final step is nearing, my thoughts are with you, but there remains no other way out.

I have fully committed myself to a great idea – fate has willed this end. I am convinced that in any event my mission will bear fruit. Maybe, in spite of my death or because of it, peace will be the result of my flight.

These pages will also be a last salute to my friends, to the General [Professor Karl Haushofer] and to Gerl [Professor Franz Gerl] and son. For you and Buz and my parents, the Führer will provide.

With all my heart, your remembering,
Rudolf

Sooner or later we all have to die. Honour to the one who dies for a great ideal![19]

The third letter was the completion of the one written to his son 'Buz' from 10 to 15 June 1941, as described in Chapter Four. This ended with the words:

Buz! Take notice. There are higher, more fateful powers, which I must point out to you – let us call them higher powers – who intervene, at least when it is time for great events. I *had* to come to England to talk about an agreement and peace. Often we do not understand these hard decisions immediately; in time to come their meaning will be clearly understood.[20]

At 04.00 hours on the morning of 16 June, Hess called for assistance. When the door was unlocked, he brushed past an officer and a sergeant and vaulted over the banisters to the stone floor of the entrance hall below. He might have broken his neck but instead landed on his feet and fractured his upper left femur. He groaned and shouted for morphia. The staff wrapped him in blankets and made him as comfortable as possible until a surgical specialist, Major C.S.J. Murray, arrived at 05.30 hours. He was given an anaesthetic, his leg was put in a splint, and he was carried back to his bedroom. It was discovered later that the bone was splintered, with deformity of the lower part. The injury kept him immobilized and in bed for twelve weeks while his leg remained in traction. Even when this was removed, he was kept in bed for another six weeks. It was not until late October that he was allowed up on crutches, with a gradual increase of weight-bearing, until he could walk normally once more without trace of disability.[21]

Hess had left two notes on the table in his room before this attempt at suicide. One requested that his uniform be handed to the Duke of Hamilton, to be sent to his family in Germany after the war. The other referred to his belief that he was being poisoned and stated that he could not resist the 'chemical war against his nerves'. He was very morose for several days afterwards, groaning with despair. On the night of the following day, he called for whisky, although he was normally a teetotaller. He grabbed the bottle when the orderly was adding water to the glass, and attempted to drink it neat. By this time he was allowed to read *The Times* each day but took little interest in the newspaper until later expressing disappointment because his broken leg was not reported.[22]

It was perhaps fortunate for Britain's prestige worldwide that Hess's action did not result in his death. However, it is apparent that either he broke his promise to Hitler about never committing suicide or else he was lying when he wrote to the duke stating that he had made the promise. He came under the care of a psychiatrist, Captain Munro Johnson of the Royal Army Medical Corps, who reported that he was suffering from paranoia and warned that another attempt at suicide would be made when he had recovered from his injury.[23]

On 22 June, six days after this attempt at suicide, Germany invaded Russia. Hess took great interest in the Press reports but it seems that he did not resume writing letters until 7 August 1941, when he wrote to his wife Ilse once more, without mentioning his injury. Eight days later he wrote to her again and enclosed a letter to his former adjutant, as follows:

Dear Pintsch,

Among other rumours I have heard that you were arrested in connection with my flight. I hope and assume that this is not correct, but if it is the case – which would be very painful to me – I beg you to look upon it as a decision of destiny and as part of an endeavour which I am convinced had to be made.

Whatever the case, I thank you for your loyalty and for your silence – otherwise I should not have been able to carry out my flight.

I wish you well especially if, I assume, you are at the front.

To our meeting in good health.

Heil Hitler!

Your

R.[24]

Hess was correct in his assumption that Pintsch paid for his silence by being sent to the Eastern Front. He was captured by the Russians at the end of the war but survived cruel treatment and eventually repatriated to

Germany on 16 December 1955. Other letters sent by Hess at this time were addressed to his parents, his brother Alfred, and Karl Haushofer. He also received letters from his wife, who sometimes wrote in the guise of their son 'Buz', pretending that the little boy was sitting on her knee and typing the letters. Hess replied in like manner, sometimes addressing his son as 'Buz' and sometimes 'Buzerich'. All these letters were affectionate in tone and concentrated on family affairs, without any evidence of the psychological disturbances which he exhibited to his guards.

On 9 September 1941 Hess received a short visit from Lord Beaverbrook, the former Minister of Aircraft Production, who was given the pseudonym 'Dr Livingstone'. Beaverbrook had met Hess in Berlin before the war but their talk on this occasion lasted only one hour. The main subject was Germany's assault on Russia, when Hess asserted that the main purpose of his flight was to persuade Britain to join with Germany in preventing the Bolsheviks from overrunning the rest of Europe.

A month later Hess learnt that his father Fritz had died on 2 October 1941, according to a German radio bulletin. Of course he wrote to his mother and also to Ilse. Reading books and newspapers seems to have been his main occupation for the next few months, but he also wrote many letters. Most of these were quite cheerful in tone, apart from a long letter he sent to King George VI on 13 November 1941, complaining about his treatment. He must have learnt of the Japanese attack on Pearl Harbor on 7 December 1941, Germany's declaration of war against the USA, and the spreading of the war to a worldwide conflict.

On 25 January 1942 the Pioneer Corps took over the duties of the Guards Regiment at Mytchett Place, a change that Hess considered less prestigious. His behaviour became even more erratic in this period. On

3 March he was reported to have 'come out of his coma or blackout, which lasted several weeks'.[25] However, this apparent amnesia did not affect his ability to write perfectly lucid letters during this period, including one to his secretary, Hildegard Fath, sending birthday wishes. It is possible that he was deliberately accentuating his mental disorders in the knowledge that if declared insane he would have to be repatriated under the terms of the Geneva Convention. Meanwhile, the officers of his guards seem to have been kind and tolerant, trying to soothe and humour him by pandering to his wishes in minor ways. They did not seem to have disliked him, and indeed some became quite friendly with him.

However, this state of affairs could not last indefinitely, for about 150 men were required to guard Mytchett Place, if only to shield their prisoner from assassination or from prying journalists. On 26 June 1942 Hess was moved to Maindiff Court Hospital near Abergavenny in South Wales. This was a former mental hospital which had been taken over by the War Office as an ordinary hospital for service personnel. It was far more secure than Mytchett Place and quarters were found for Hess in two small rooms. He was still allowed newspapers and could even go for walks or drives in the countryside, suitably guarded. His mental health as a prisoner had always come under the overall care of Brigadier J.R. Rees, the Consulting Psychiatrist to the Army, who paid him a number of visits at both Mytchett Place and Maindiff Court. On 29 September 1942 Dr Rees reported that Hess was tense and strained, depressed at the news of the fighting at Stalingrad and suffering abdominal cramps. He was still unsure whether he was being poisoned and Rees assessed him as 'a paranoid person of a psychopathic type who has definite hysterical and hypochondrical tendencies'.[26] In October 1943 Hess resumed faking amnesia, or at least stressed genuine loss of memory brought about by mental disorder. He also took the precaution of stating that his memory was going, in a letter to his wife dated 7 March 1944.[27] His behaviour continued to puzzle his guards throughout the year.

Hess was unaware that an astonishing plan involving him was put forward by the Special Operations Executive (SOE) in late 1944. This was part of Operation *Foxley*, in which the SOE's Section X (German) examined the possibilities of assassinating Hitler and other German leaders. These measures had been considered from the previous January but more definite proposals began to crystallize by June 1944, with the intention of using a small group of German and Austrian PoWs known as 'bonzos' who were being trained as armed assassins. The planning continued after the failure of the bomb plot on Hitler's life by Colonel Claus Schenk, *Graf* von Stauffenberg, on 20 July 1944.[28]

Although Hitler was the main target, Himmler was regarded as a second choice, being known as *Foxley II*. On 18 December 1944 a memorandum under *X Plans* suggested that Hess might be used as an assassin for such an operation. It was thought that he might be bluffed or hypnotized into believing that Himmler was the only person preventing peace negotiations between the Allies and Germany. Thus his elimination would bring reality to Hess's long-held dream. The planners stated that Hess was known to be an extremely nervous individual and should be very susceptible to hypnotic treatment. The proposal was put forward again on 8 January 1945, but on this occasion Hess's sanity and physical fitness were queried.[29] However, none of these plans was authorized, partly since there was a reluctance to make martyrs of the German leaders and partly since it was realized that Hitler's ineptitude as a military commander was helping the Allies to win the war.

Hess's bizarre behaviour at Maindiff Court continued

and Rees warned that there was 'still the risk of further attempted suicide'. This occurred in the afternoon of 4 February 1945 when Hess stabbed himself in the lower left side of the chest with a bread knife, after telling a doctor that his memory had returned. It was an ineffectual attempt, requiring no more than a couple of stitches, but he refused food afterwards, saying that he would starve himself to death. He relented four days later but remained morose. The reasons for this acute depression are not hard to seek, for by this time Allied troops were advancing steadily over German soil and the remains of the war-making capacity of the country were being destroyed by Allied bombing. It was apparent, even to Hess, that the war was lost and that his beloved idol, Adolf Hitler, would end in a hangman's noose if captured.

In the first months of 1945 the final disintegration of the Third Reich took place. Albrecht Haushofer, Hess's mentor on the subject of the Duke of Hamilton, was executed by the SS in Berlin on 23 April 1945. Adolf Hitler killed himself in Berlin a week later, and Germany finally capitulated. During the following July Hess began to complain once more about loss of memory, although the doctors responded with some scepticism. He remained in Maindiff Court but orders were received on 6 October to remove him to Nuremberg. He was flown there four days later, taking off from Madley near Hereford and with a short stop at Brussels.[30]

Hess's fate was to appear before an International Military Tribunal with twenty-two other prominent Nazis who could be indicted on four counts. These were 'Common Plan or Conspiracy', 'Crimes against Peace', 'War Crimes' and 'Crimes against Humanity'. The last two were not levelled against Hess, since he had been a prisoner in Britain at the time most of these were committed, but he was arraigned on the first two.

The proceedings of the Four Powers (Britain, France,

Russia and the USA) opened on 20 November. Hess was found fit to plead, although he had pretended that he could not even remember Goering or his secretary Hildegard Fath. He appeared to show little interest in the case until ten days later when asked if he wanted to speak. At this point he astonished everyone by stating that his memory had returned, although he did not recognize the jurisdiction of the Court. The case against him began on 7 February 1946 and, together with the other proceedings, dragged on until the end of the following September, when judgments were given against all defendants. One had committed suicide before the trials began, three were acquitted, twelve were sentenced to be hanged, four were sentenced to long terms of imprisonment and three, including Hess, were sentenced to life imprisonment. Meanwhile Albrecht's parents, Karl and Martha Haushofer, had committed suicide on 11 March 1946, although the old professor had not been arrested by the Allies.

The seven Nazis sentenced to imprisonment remained in Nuremberg until 18 July 1947, when they were flown in a Dakota from Fürth airfield to RAF Gatow near Berlin and transferred to the Allied military prison at Wilhelmstrasse 23 in Spandau. This was the last occasion during his lifetime when Hess entered any aircraft, either military or civil, for he was incarcerated in Spandau prison until his death, although he sometimes visited a military hospital in Berlin for medical treatment.

The prison was closely guarded, each of the Four Powers taking its turn for a period of a month. There were six watch-towers and an electrified barbed-wire fence, and the whole prison was floodlit at night. The exterior guard consisted of 32 soldiers and in addition there were 18 warders and 38 auxiliary staff. A strict regime had been set out by the Control Commission in Nuremberg. The prisoners were required to stand before all officers and warders, to salute them and obey all orders and regulations without question. They were addressed only by number and never by name, Hess being No. 7. They were locked up in individual cells and not allowed to address each other. They were required to work and clean their cells. However, walks and religious services were carried out together.[31]

According to the distinguished German historian Werner Maser, Hess was temporarily released from his cell on the night of 17/18 March 1952, at a time when the Russians were guarding Spandau. Without the knowledge of the Western Powers, he was taken to a secret location where he met senior officials of the German Democratic Republic. On Stalin's instructions he was offered his freedom and a leading position in that country, provided he declared that it was realizing the socialist ideal to which he had always aspired. However, Hess remained true to his idol, Hitler, and turned down this offer, to the fury of the Russians. They warned him against revealing anything about this outing and declared that he would remain in Spandau until his death.[32] If this episode occurred, the prisoner took the secret to his grave.

Hess's mother Klara died on 1 October 1951, without having seen her son since before his flight to Scotland. All the prisoners save Hess were released in turn, some before the ends of their sentences on grounds of age and health, including the two others serving life sentences. One of the latter was Grand Admiral Erich Raeder, who had been convicted on three counts; he was released on 26 September 1955. The other was Walther Funk, the former President of the Reichsbank, who had also been convicted on three counts; he was released on 16 May 1957.

By 30 December 1966 Rudolf Hess, who had been convicted on only two counts, remained the sole prisoner in Spandau. He eventually outlived all the six prisoners who had been released. His brother Alfred also died, on 9

June 1963. Meanwhile, he refused any visit from his family. It was not until 24 December 1969, when he was in the British Military Hospital for treatment to a perforated duodenal ulcer, that he allowed his wife Ilse and their architect son Wolf Rüdiger to see him, for the first time since 10 May 1941. Thereafter they visited him on many occasions, although as the years wore on Ilse became too frail to make the journey. Wolf Rüdiger campaigned tirelessly for the release of his father, supported by many appeals from international bodies and influential individuals, but the Soviet authorities blocked all his attempts. Hess tried to take his life once more, by cutting his wrists with a knife on 22 February 1977, but the attempt was not successful.

In Hess's period as a solitary prisoner, the spartan conditions in Spandau were steadily improved under pressure of world opinion. His final years were far less harsh than the public was led to believe. He did not live in solitary confinement and was allowed to move freely within all the cells in the block allocated to him. He could talk to any warder or the medical orderly on duty. From 1982 the permanent medical orderly was a Tunisian, Abdallah Melaouhi, who was married to a German woman and spoke both French and German. This man looked after Hess very conscientiously, to the point of pampering. He lived just outside the main gate and was on constant call, unless he was on leave when another male nurse stood in for him. The heating in Hess's cell was adjusted to whatever temperature he preferred. He set his own routine, rising at whatever time he wished. Two cooks were employed specially for him and prepared the dishes he selected. His appetite remained huge and he ate an enormous amount of food. Selected newspapers were provided. Wall-to-wall carpeting was fitted in his bedroom and the television room. A shower and safety grips were fitted in his bathroom. Clothing was tailored for him. A film projector was installed so that he could watch home movies, and a record player was provided for his preference of classical music. A special lift was installed to take him to his garden, so he no longer had to walk up and down the spiral staircase. He spent most of his time reading, gardening, watching television and taking a keen interest in space exploration.[33]

Hess was allowed to receive one letter a week from his family and to write one in return, although these were subject to censorship. Other incoming mail, such as that from neo-Nazi groups, was shredded. Some television programmes were supposed to be forbidden, although he could easily circumvent this regulation with the remote control. A chaplain could visit him once a week. He was allowed one visit a month from a single family member, with two visits in December. He seems to have established a special rapport with his daughter-in-law Andrea, who provided photographs and home movies of his grand-children.[34]

On 17 August 1987 the world media reported that Rudolf Hess had died, at the age of ninety-three. Three days later his body was taken from the British Military Hospital in Berlin to RAF Gatow and flown by Lockheed Hercules C.1 serial XV297 of the RAF to the US airfield at Grafenwöhr, about 40 km south of Wunsiedel, where it was handed over to his family for burial. The circumstances of his death remained confused until the Four Powers issued a joint statement on 17 September:

1.   The Four Powers are now in a position to make a final statement on the death of Rudolf Hess.
2.   Investigations have confirmed that on 17 August Rudolf Hess hanged himself from a window latch in a small summer house in the prison garden, using an electrical extension cord which had for some time been kept in the summer house for use in connection with a

reading lamp. Attempts were made to revive him and he was then rushed to the British Military Hospital where, after further unsuccessful attempts to resuscitate him, he was pronounced dead at 16.10.

3.  A note addressed to Hess's family was found in his pocket. This note was written on the reverse side of a letter from his daughter-in-law [Andrea Hess] dated 20 July 1987. It began with the words 'Please would the Governors send this home. Written a few minutes before my death.' The senior document examiner from the laboratory of the British Government Chemist, Mr P.A.M. Beard, has examined the note, and concluded that he can see no reason to doubt that it was written by Rudolf Hess.

4.  A full autopsy was performed on Hess's body on 19 August in the British Military Hospital by Dr J. Malcolm Cameron. The autopsy was conducted in the presence of medical representatives of the Four Powers. The report noted a linear mark on the left side of the neck consistent with a ligature. Dr Cameron stated that in his opinion death resulted from asphyxia, caused by compression of the neck due to suspension.

5.  The investigations confirmed that the routine followed by staff on the day of Hess's suicide was consistent with normal practice. Hess had tried to cut his wrists with a table knife in 1977. Immediately after this incident warders were placed in his room and he was watched 24 hours a day. This was discontinued after several months as impracticable, unnecessary and an inappropriate invasion of Hess's privacy.

A translation of the remainder of the note written by Hess is:

I thank all my loved ones for all that you have done for me. Tell Freiburg I was extremely sorry that I had to behave ever since the Nuremberg Trials as if I did not

know her. There was nothing else I could do, since otherwise all attempts to free me would have been useless. I had looked forward to seeing her again. I have received photographs of her as well as of all of you.
Your Big One.

The name Freiburg referred to his secretary, Hildegard Fath, whom he had refused to recognize when he simulated amnesia at the beginning of his trial. Meanwhile his body was buried temporarily in a secret location, to avoid attention from the media or any demonstrations from members of the public with residual Nazi sympathies. It was later exhumed and reinterred quietly on 17 March 1988 in the family plot at Wunsiedel. The headstone bears the words ICH HAB'S GEWAGT, meaning 'I dared'. He was survived by his wife Ilse, who died on 7 September 1995 at the age of ninety-five and was buried beside him.

Rudolf Hess was kept in prison for over forty-six years. This long incarceration was considered by many to be contrary to the standards of humanity in any civilized community. Well before his death, the man who was classed as the bitterest enemy of the Nazi creed in the Second World War gave his opinion on this matter. This was Winston Churchill, who wrote:

I am glad not to be responsible for the way in which Hess has been and is being treated. Whatever may be the moral guilt of a German who stood near to Hitler, Hess had, in my view, atoned for this by his completely devoted and frantic deed of lunatic benevolence. He came to us of his own free will and, though without authority, had something of the quality of an envoy. He was a medical and not a criminal case and should be so regarded.[35]

# CHAPTER EIGHT

# *Some of the Myths*

The unexpected release of Foreign Office papers relating to Hess by the Public Record Office in 1991, 1992, 1998 and 1999 has proved a serious blow to the conspiracy theorists. The first two batches contained nothing to support any of their hypotheses. Similarly, the papers of the Special Operations Executive (SOE) which became available in July 1998, some of which related to Hess, do nothing to help their various theories. Finally, the Second World War papers from MI5, which became available to the public in January 1999, contain an enquiry into the flight of Rudolf Hess which flatly contradicts most of these conspiracy theories.[1]

Until then, some of these authors had been able to assert with confidence that their theories would be substantiated when certain official papers were released, at a date expected to be 2017. Now that the files have become available, these authors are in an awkward and embarrassing situation. It is abundantly clear to impartial researchers that the documents simply confirm the more rational and commonsense explanation for Hess's flight to Britain: the decision was made by himself and himself alone.

The conspiracy theories are many and various. For simplicity, it may be advisable to examine some of them under headings.

## THE DUKE OF HAMILTON WAS ASSOCIATED WITH HESS AND IMPLICATED IN HIS FLIGHT

The first in this field were several Communists. These included Harry Pollitt, the general secretary of the British

Communist Party, who had been sentenced in 1925 to twelve months' imprisonment for sedition and libel. Another was H. Goodman, the publisher of a journal entitled *World News and Views*, who distributed a pamphlet asserting that Hamilton and Hess were friends and that the duke approved of the Hitlerian regime. Hamilton brought a libel action against these Communists. The case was heard in the High Court of Justice on 18 February 1942, and in the absence of any evidence the defendants had no option but to withdraw and apologize publicly.[2] However, the more modern conspiracy theorists do not have this legal hindrance, since the duke died on 30 March 1973 at the age of seventy and can no longer defend himself.

One of the difficulties in refuting such an allegation is that the authors have produced nothing to support it other than their own suspicions. In legal terms 'there is no case to answer'. It is true that the duke hoped to avoid a war between Britain and Germany, before he realized that the menace of the Nazis was real. He was a schoolboy during the First World War but everyone of his generation had had personal experience of the appalling waste of life in that conflict and the grief it brought to so many families. People of good will were aghast at the prospect of this colossal tragedy repeating itself. But it is absolutely clear that both before and during the war, Hamilton served his country loyally with all the powers at his disposal.

The duke was the eldest of four brothers serving in the RAF. The second was Wing Commander Lord Nigel 'Geordie' Douglas-Hamilton OBE AFC, later the Earl of Selkirk. He had commanded 603 (City of Edinburgh) Squadron, an Auxiliary Air Force squadron, from October 1938 to August 1939. At the time of Hess's flight, he was working in the Air Ministry as a deputy director of flying training. The third was Wing Commander Lord Malcolm Douglas-Hamilton, who was working with the Air Staff in Salisbury, Southern Rhodesia, developing the Rhodesian

Air Training Group, a highly successful part of Britain's Empire Air Training Scheme. Later in the war, from May 1943 to March 1944, he commanded one of the RAF's famous photo-reconnaissance squadrons, No. 540, at a time when it was equipped with Mosquitos. The youngest was Flying Officer Lord David Douglas-Hamilton, who was a flying instructor at the beginning of the war. From December 1941 to March 1943 he also commanded 603 Squadron, at a time when it was based in Malta and equipped with Spitfire VBs. He later became a flight commander in 544 Squadron, another famous photo-reconnaissance squadron equipped with Mosquitos, but tragically lost his life in a crash on 2 August 1944 when struggling back to base on one engine from a sortie to the Dijon area.

The eldest brother of this eminent and patriotic family, the Duke of Hamilton, had no sympathy with the Nazi cause, nor was he part of an anti-government faction as Hess mistakenly believed. He belonged to the same political party as Winston Churchill and was on terms of personal friendship with him. His only link with Hess was an extremely tenuous one. He had offered hospitality to Albrecht Haushofer, the part-Jewish and anti-Nazi son of Dr Karl Haushofer, who in turn was one of Hess's friends and mentors. Although Hess was undoubtedly a very skilful and resourceful pilot and navigator, his grasp of the nature of British politics and its personalities was seriously defective. In his confused state of mind, he had picked a man who would never have helped him in his quest.

## BRITISH MILITARY INTELLIGENCE INDUCED HESS TO MAKE HIS FLIGHT

It was the Russians who first propounded this belief. Stalin had not believed an urgent warning from the British in April 1941 about Hitler's intention of attacking his country. Moreover, when the assault began on 22 June 1941, he became convinced that Britain was in league with Germany in an attempt to destroy his country, and that Hess's flight had been engineered by British intelligence with the Duke of Hamilton as a go-between. This suspicion persisted even after Britain did its best to bring war supplies to Russia with their Arctic convoys to Archangel. The Russians could not understand why Britain did not prosecute Hess as a war criminal but kept him in comfortable quarters as a prisoner-of-war to await a post-war trial. Their suspicions reached a ridiculous stage on 19 October 1942 when the official newspaper of the Communist Party in the USSR, *Pravda* (*Truth*), stated:

It is no coincidence that Hess's wife has asked certain British representatives if she could join her husband. This could mean that she does not see her husband as a prisoner. It is high time we knew whether Hess is either a criminal or a plenipotentiary who represents the Nazi government in England.

A few days later the newspaper published a photograph of 'Mrs Hess' giving a piano recital in London. This turned out to be Myra Hess, the celebrated concert pianist who enthralled Londoners and boosted wartime morale by playing at lunchtimes to packed houses in the National Gallery.[3] The Russian intelligence service seems to have reached a remarkable stage of ineptitude.

Stalin persisted in his belief when Churchill visited Moscow to discuss matters of importance and had a late farewell supper with Stalin at the Kremlin of 01.00 hours on 18 October 1944. Also present were the British Foreign Secretary, Anthony Eden, and the Russian Foreign Minister, Molotov. One of the many matters on the agenda was the flight of Rudolf Hess, and Churchill said he would 'reconstruct the workings of Hess's mind'. He said that

Hess was jealous of the German generals, loved Hitler and had become crazy, thinking he could 'save England for Germany'. After getting hold of an aircraft and flying to Britain, he tried to explain his ideas to the Duke of Hamilton and asked to see the king. He was then put into prison and threw himself over some banisters in a half-hearted attempt at suicide and broke his thigh. Churchill finished by saying that Hess had become completely mad and that his relations with Hitler were probably abnormal. Stalin responded unexpectedly by proposing a toast to the British Intelligence Service which had 'inveigled Hess into coming to Britain'. Churchill protested, evidently in vain, that the British Government had known nothing about the journey in advance.[4]

These wartime Russian beliefs resurfaced on 7 June 1991 when information about Hess was released via Colonel Oleg I. Tsarev, the deputy head of the First Department of the KGB in Moscow. By this time, however, the emphasis had shifted. The KGB asserted that the Duke of Hamilton was not directly involved but that faked letters purporting to come from him were sent to Hess by MI6, with the intention of luring him to Britain. According to the KGB this information came from Kim Philby, a British agent who was one of the 'Cambridge Five' group of traitors secretly working for Russian intelligence. Philby was stated to have obtained this information from his old friend Tom Dupree, the deputy chief of the Foreign Office's press department, and passed it to his Soviet controllers on 22 May 1941.[5]

It has to be assumed that the Russians are referring to the period between the letter written by Albrecht Haushofer on 23 September 1940 to the Duke of Hamilton, inviting him to a meeting in Portugal, and mid-March 1941 when British intelligence made the letter available to the duke. However, Hess makes no mention of such a lure in the documents released by the Public Record Office, while the Duke of Hamilton was unaware of any faked letters sent under his name. Philby did not include this matter in his book *My Secret War*, in which he boasted of his many achievements as a spy for the Russians and sought to sow discord among British and American intelligence agents. It can be shown that he was such an inveterate liar that even the Russians did not fully trust him after he fled to the Soviet Union in January 1963. In the period before Hess's flight and early imprisonment, Philby was working at an SOE training school at Beaulieu in Hampshire and had no direct access to any MI6 information.

There is some evidence which points to the falsehood of these statements. The wartime records of MI6 are housed in the Foreign Office, and the political head of this department of state is the Foreign Secretary. On 2 December 1973 the Foreign Secretary, Sir Alec Douglas-Home, arrived in Moscow for talks with his Russian counterpart, Andrei Gromyko. In the course of this, he pleaded with the Russians for an agreement to release Hess from Spandau by his eightieth birthday, 26 April 1974. The Russians remained adamant and this request was refused.[6] It seems extremely unlikely that Douglas-Home would have taken this action if the Foreign Office had been harbouring some dark secret which Hess might have divulged on his release. Even if Douglas-Home had not read the files in the past, he is likely to have requested the relevant information from the Division Head of the Department, who had access to all the material. But the relevant MI6 records for the Second World War have not been released to the public and are unlikely to be made available for many years.

## HESS MADE HIS FLIGHT WITH HITLER'S KNOWLEDGE AND WAS ACTING AS HIS EMISSARY

This is another theory based on assumptions rather than on positive evidence. There can be little doubt that the German authorities were aware of Hess's general activities at Augsburg-Haunstetten airfield. It would have been impossible to have kept his flying practice secret when so many pilots, mechanics and other ground staff were directly involved in the circumstances. During a period when all Nazis in Germany were encouraged to report on anyone else if they thought fit, Hess's obsession with aircraft and flying must have been well known to the Gestapo. This is verified by the German broadcast of 12 May 1941 which stated 'On Saturday 10 May, around 18.00 hours, Hess stook off *again* [authors' italics] from Augsburg.' Although the word 'again' does not appear in the British translation of the broadcast, it is in the Dutch translation (*weer*) for 13 May. The word *äter* (again) also appears in the neutral Swedish Press.[7]

If Hitler learnt of his deputy's flying activities, he took no steps to stop them. Hess had been a keen aviator since the First World War and had promised Hitler that he would refrain from further flying for only a year after September 1939. He was not playing a major part in the conduct of the war and Hitler had far more important matters on his mind than denying him this pleasure, which seemed innocent enough.

The real evidence that Hitler knew nothing of Hess's intention of flying to Scotland is available from several sources. First, Hess himself was adamant in his statements to the British that he had flown entirely on his own initiative. Secondly, he wrote to his adjutant, Karlheinz Pintsch, thanking him for remaining silent and stating that otherwise he would not have been able to make his historic flight. Thirdly, the experienced and sagacious statesman

Lord Simon became convinced that Hess was making his own interpretation of Hitler's peace requirements, partly since he became uncertain when pressed for further details. Fourthly, there is the evidence from Albert Speer, who witnessed Hitler's almost uncontrollable rage when he learnt of Hess's flight. Fifthly, there is the evidence in Josef Goebbel's diaries to the effect that Hitler said Hess deserved to be shot for his treasonable flight.

Lastly, there are the results of an investigation carried out by MI5 in Germany after the war. This report is dated 12 March 1946 but was not released to the public until January 1999.[8] It stated that members of Hess's entourage who were arrested after his flight to Scotland included his adjutants as well as Professor Karl Haushofer, Professor Albrecht Haushofer, the astrologer Dr Ernst Schulte-Strathaus and Professor Dr Franz Gerl.

The MI5 investigation concluded that Hess had flown to Scotland on his own initiative and without any orders from Hitler. It also confirmed that Hess had left a letter for Hitler and that this had been handed to the Führer by his adjutants. Hess had stated in his letter that he hoped to obtain a last-minute understanding with Britain before the commencement of the German offensive against the USSR on 22 June 1941.

Two people who had had great influence on Hess were Karl Haushofer and his son Albrecht, whose theories had weighed heavily with him in his plans. Another person of influence was Dr Schulte-Strathaus, who had cast horoscopes for him on numerous occasions. In the last instance, made at the end of April 1941, this astrologer had forecast that the signs were propitious for Hess in the following month. Hess had accepted this prognostication and acted accordingly.

The adjutants had known of Hess's trial flights from Augsburg-Haustetten and were also aware that these were forbidden by Hitler. Thus the men had been imprisoned until 1942, when they were discharged and sent to the fighting front. Dr Schulte-Strathaus had also been imprisoned for a period, but the Haushofers and Dr Gerl (a close friend of Hess's, to whom he wrote while imprisoned in Britain) had been released after being arrested during the investigation.

All mail leaving Germany for Hess had been censored, especially letters from his wife. A case file on Hess had been built up by the SS and a final report submitted to Hitler, but this had been deliberately destroyed in April 1945.[9] This recently released MI5 investigation and report tallies closely with all other reliable evidence in this matter.

A new variant on the conspiracy theories was advanced by the authors John Harris and M.J. Trow in their book entitled *Hess: The British Conspiracy* published in early 1999. These authors express the belief that Hess was induced to fly to Scotland by four members of Special Operations 1, part of the British Secret Service, and that he did so with the knowledge of Hitler. He was not heading for Dungavel but for either RAF Acklington or an RAF airstrip at Lennoxlove, where he had been led to believe that a peace party would be waiting for him. His flight over Northumberland and Scotland was made in a hunt for these objectives.

Among the oddities in this book, the authors refer to the MI5 documents released to the public in January 1999 with the comment: 'However, there was nothing in the files that actually detailed the series of events leading to the flight.'[10] They appear to have overlooked the official MI5 enquiry detailed above. Another curious statement is that their researchers were bedevilled by the difficulty of obtaining details of the contents of Hess's pockets, probably contained in document WO 199/3288B 'which will remain classified until 2017'.[11] In fact, this document was released in 1991, eight years before their book was published. It concerns letters relating to Hess's medical condition while in Scotland. The contents of Hess's pockets are in FO 1093/10, another document the authors seem to have missed, and are mainly of interest for the homeopathic medicines he brought with him.

## HESS COULD NOT HAVE FLOWN OVER GERMAN TERRITORY WITHOUT AUTHORISATION

This is the type of statement made by authors with extremely limited knowledge of flying in the Second World War. The truth is that aircraft with German markings could fly unhindered almost anywhere over their own territory, in the same way that RAF aircraft could fly over Britain. There were certain prohibited zones such as major cities or ports, but an aircraft would not be challenged or fired upon if it kept clear of these. In the days when radar was directed solely towards enemy territory, there was no reliable method of tracking friendly aircraft on internal flights. At any one time there were hundreds of aircraft criss-crossing the country, on operational or training flights, and no one would hunt for them unless they were reported as missing. The Germans did not have a civilian network of posts, such as those of the Royal Observer Corps, to make visual sightings of aircraft. Instead, there was a huge anti-aircraft organization, known as the *Flak* (short for *Fliegerabwehrkanone*) arm, which was in three parts. The German army and navy had their own *Flak* units, but by far the largest came under the Luftwaffe. This mustered about a million men at the outbreak of war. All these gunners were trained rigorously in aircraft recognition and could easily identify the well-known Messerschmitt Bf110. They would never have fired on one of their own aircraft unless specifically ordered to do so.

Similarly, German pilots could recognize their own aircraft and their markings. If Pintsch had reported Hess's intention soon after he took off, it might have been possible for fighters to intercept the Bf110. Even then, they would have had to close up sufficiently to recognize the radio code VJ+OQ on the side of the machine before taking action. Then they would either have buzzed it sufficiently aggressively to persuade Hess to land somewhere or else have shot it down. But according to Adolf Galland, the news of Hess's flight did not reach Goering until Hess was over the North Sea and beyond their reach.

When Hess had passed over German territory and come within range of the outward-looking German radar, he would have been able to rely on a device known as FuG 25. This was similar to the RAF's IFF (Identification, Friend or Foe) which provided a different shaped blip on the radar screen, enabling the German operators to identify his aircraft as one of their own.

## HESS MADE AN INTERMEDIATE LANDING AT SCHIPHOL AIRPORT, NEAR AMSTERDAM

This story originated from the American Consul in Amsterdam, James H. Lord, who wrote a long report when he left the country in August 1941. Parts were marked 'rumour', 'reliable' or 'probably correct'. In one part he wrote:

> On the best authority I can report that Hess landed at Schiphol Airport to have his plane refuelled. The airport authorities [had] received a phone call from Augsburg to refuel Hess's Bf110.

He then continued by saying that he did not know if the authorities at Schiphol knew the identity of the pilot.[12]

This report is contradictory, for in one part Lord states that the authorities were informed that Hess was flying the aircraft and in another that they did not know the identity of the pilot. He does not quote the source of his information, so it is impossible to check its veracity. However, the control tower log books of Schiphol airport can be checked, and there is no mention of Hess's machine or of any Bf110 landing there on 10 May 1941. They do include the taking off of three Junkers Ju88s of *Kampfgeschwader 77* and two more from *Küstenfliegergruppe 106*, indicating that the pages of the log are complete.[13]

In fact, there was intensive security at the airport at the time. Five days earlier two Dutchmen had managed to escape in a twin-engined Fokker G-1 long-range fighter originally put into production for the Royal Netherlands Air Force. These were a test pilot, Hidde Leegstra, and an engineer, Pieter Jan Cornelis Vos, both of whom had pretended to be sympathetic to the Nazi cause. A Fokker G-1 was being prepared for delivery to the Luftwaffe and the two Dutchmen promised to perform some aerobatics in it during the early evening. Once in the air, they headed for England and made a safe landing in a field at South Cove, near the coast of Suffolk.[14] After this, the Germans at Schiphol airport were in serious trouble and monitored the movements of all aircraft very carefully.

Quite apart from the intensive security at Schiphol, there was no need for Hess to land and refuel. As can be seen from Appendices F and G of this book, his machine was quite capable of making the flight with the fuel put into its tanks at Augsburg-Haunstetten. His own record of the flight, as written to his son between 10 to 15 June 1941, shows that he must have passed about 80 km east of the airport. A diversion from his planned track would have upset his careful calculations, created an unnecessary waste of time and endangered his mission.

## HESS TOOK OFF FROM CALAIS AND NOT AUGSBURG

This story became current when the Swedish newspaper *Svenska Dagbladet* published a report on 23 May 1941 as follows:

> It is not correct that Hess started from Augsburg, or any other place in Germany. He took off from Calais, which explains how he reached Scotland.[15]

According to this report the information originated from London, and thus must have come from one of the newspaper's reporters. It is, of course, completely fallacious, as can be verified from both German and British records. No such statement was ever issued from official sources, and one can only conclude that the newspaper reporter had spoken to someone who mistakenly believed that Hess's machine did not have the range to reach Scotland from Augsburg and made an incorrect guess at its point of departure.

## HESS WAS ESCORTED FOR PART OF HIS FLIGHT BY REINHARD HEYDRICH

This is suggested by the author Peter Padfield in his book *Hess: Flight for the Führer*. The primary source was Heydrich's widow, who wrote a memoir after the war stating that her husband was 'residing' on the Channel coast at this time and flying Messerschmitt Bf109s towards England.[16] Reinhard Heydrich, nicknamed 'The Hangman', was head of the *Reichssicherheitshauptampt* (Main Central Security Office), a service which included the sadistic Gestapo. It seemed unlikely to Peter Padfield that he would be allowed to risk his life in the air without some special purpose. Thus he postulated that

Heydrich's role was to protect Hess on his flight. This reinforced his contention that Hess flew to England with the approval of Hitler.

However, if one examines the known facts about Heydrich, a very different light is thrown on the subject of his flying career. Born on 7 March 1904, he was too young to have served in the First World War. He joined the German Navy in 1922 but was court-martialled in 1931 and dismissed for having an affair with a young girl. He joined the SS in 1932 and became a prominent member, rising to the rank of general in 1941. Meanwhile, he had become a skilled aerobatic pilot between the wars, flying light aircraft. He owned a Heinkel He72B Kadett (Cadet), registration D-EAKY, a two-seat biplane similar to the de Havilland Tiger Moth used for initial training.

In September 1939 Goering gave Heydrich the honorary rank of major in the Luftwaffe. Heydrich's first operational experience was as an air gunner in Heinkel He111s of *Kampfgeschwader 55* during the invasion of Poland. Later in 1939 he entered *Jagdfliegerschule* (Fighter Pilots' School) 1 at Werneuchen, north-east of Berlin, where he trained on Messerschmitt Bf109s. In April and May 1940 he served with *6./Jagdgeschwader 77* at Stavanger-Sola airfield in Norway and in fact crashed a Bf109E-1 there on 13 May, without injury to himself. He returned to Werneuchen in April 1941. In early May 1941 he served with *I./Jagdgeschwader 1*, not on the Channel coast but at De Kooy, an airfield near Den Helder in the Netherlands, flying Bf109s on coastal defence missions. In July 1941 he joined *II./Jagdgeschwader 77*, against Himmler's orders, and took part in the advance of the Wehrmacht into Russia. He was shot down by Russian flak on 22 July 1941 over the Olshanka region, while flying Bf109E-7 works number 3765, but once again escaped injury after crash-landing behind German lines. This was too much for Himmler, and Heydrich was ordered to return to Berlin immediately.[17]

In short, Heydrich was an enthusiastic pilot, similar to Hess but younger, and for part of the first two years of the war was able to combine operational flying in the Luftwaffe with his other activities. There are no German records to substantiate the theory that he escorted Hess on part of his flight to Scotland, or indeed that he flew over the North Sea on that day. Peter Padfield states that Heydrich was 'lost for words' when asked what would have happened if he had shot down Hess on his flight. This is the only part of his hypothesis which rings true. Heydrich himself was never able to refute this fanciful story more positively, for on 27 May 1942 he was wounded by a grenade thrown by Czech patriots while he was riding in his car at Holesovice on his way from Prague to the airport at Jenec, at a time when he was *Reichsprotektor* for Bohemia and Moravia, and died in hospital on 4 June.

## THE RAF AND OTHER DEFENCES WERE ORDERED NOT TO ATTACK HESS'S MESSERSCHMITT

Although it is not the most far-fetched of the theories advanced in connection with Hess's flight, this idea appears quite ludicrous to anyone who has studied the official records and has knowledge of the RAF's wartime operations. In response to such statements appearing in the national press, Wing Commander Hector H. MacLean wrote on 5 June 1991 to the editor of *The Sunday Telegraph*:

It was suggested in your article of 5th May the RAF deliberately let Hess through on the evening of 10th May 1941. This could not have been contrived without the co-operation of the Duty Controllers in the Operations Room and the Filter Room at No 13 Group, Newcastle-upon-Tyne; nor without instructions to the sector controllers at Acklington, Turnhouse and Ayr who operated our fighters. Such a thing could not have been kept secret. As duty controller of the Ayr sector I was responsible for the air defences in the West of Scotland. I was not warned . . .

MacLean continued by describing the attack he ordered on the enemy aircraft and his subsequent telephone call to the Duke of Hamilton when the German captain, the pilot of the crashed Bf110, wished to speak to him, and the duke's utter astonishment. He received a courteous reply from the editor of *The Sunday Telegraph*, Trevor Grove, stating that his material was too long for inclusion in the correspondence column. MacLean abandoned his attempt to refute this nonsensical allegation, apart from sending copies of the correspondence to one of the authors of this book.[18]

If the RAF had been ordered to allow Hess's aircraft to pass unhindered, it would have been necessary to advise Fighter Command's Headquarters as well as every area and sector controller, who in turn would have passed the orders on to their staffs in addition to the various RAF stations and squadrons. It would have been impossible to have maintained secrecy at the time or for so many years after the war.

Moreover, if Hess's aircraft had been expected, RAF fighters would have been sent up to escort it safely to its destination. It can be established quite clearly from public records that three Spitfires and a Defiant were ordered to *attack*, and not escort, the approaching enemy aircraft. On 25 July 1989 one of these Spitfire pilots, Maurice Pocock, was filmed by a television team from BBC *Timewatch* at the Imperial War Museum in London, in the presence of one of the authors of this book, who was acting in a consultancy capacity. The programme was intended to investigate the circumstances of Hess's flight to Scotland. Pocock related how he took off to hunt for the intruder and described the problem of picking out the machine in the fading light over the dark hills of Northumberland. The interviewer then asked: 'What would you have done if you'd caught up with it?' Pocock looked at him with incredulity. 'I'd have shot it down!' he snapped.

On the same occasion the team filmed the 'teller' at Fighter Command Headquarters, Felicity Ashbee, who explained that Hess's aircraft was treated as a hostile intruder, being identified as 'Raid 42'. The author was also filmed, in front of the remains of Hess's aircraft, when he pointed out that the radio code VJ+OQ clearly visible on the side of the fuselage was that of the machine which had taken off from Augsburg. None of this filming was included in the TV programme, which was shown on BBC2 in the evening of 17 January 1990, entitled *An Edge of Conspiracy*.[19]

Another proposition put forward is that the Duke of Hamilton refused to allow fighters to attack Hess's aircraft. This appears in *Ten Days That Saved The West* by John Costello, a book which contains a string of elementary errors concerning the RAF.[20] This author asserts that the duke was 'the man on the spot responsible for responding to Raid 42'. This is not true. Turnhouse was one of the sectors of No. 13 Group, but was too far from the scene of action for its fighters to intercept the enemy aircraft. Hess flew over the Ouston and Ayr sectors, where the duke had no control, and these two sectors did their best to shoot down the intruder. The duke could watch the progress of the enemy aircraft on his operations table at Turnhouse, but was unable to take part in any defensive action.

Associated with the belief that the RAF allowed Hess's aircraft to pass unhindered, John Costello states that the anti-aircraft defences in the areas over which it passed were ordered not to open fire.[21] In this instance he is correct, but not for the reason he suggests. The air defences of the United Kingdom came under the operational control of the RAF's Fighter Command, which not only issued instructions to its own groups but to the Army's Anti-Aircraft Command. When enemy aircraft were chased by RAF fighters, as was the case with Hess's aircraft, anti-aircraft batteries were invariably ordered to refrain from firing, for fear of bringing down friendly aircraft. This was a perfectly normal practice, and not confined to the arrival of Hess's aircraft. It is untrue to suggest otherwise.

Yet another report was published in *The Sunday Telegraph* of 21 February 1999. Written by Rajeev Syal, it had the imposing title 'RAF hid secret of how Czech pilots nearly killed Hess'. This is based on an assertion in a book entitled *Fighter Pilot*, written by Jiri Rajlich and published in Prague. This states that two Czechoslovakian pilots in the RAF, Sergeants Vaclav Bauman and Leopold Srom of 245 Squadron based at Aldergrove in Northern Ireland, were closing in on Hess's Messerschmitt in the 'early evening' of 10 May 1941 when they were inexplicably called off. The article states that there is no official record of their sortie and that the Commanding Officer, Squadron Leader J.W.C. Simpson, queried the matter with Fighter Command's Headquarters but was replaced within a month.

An examination of 245 Squadron's Operations Record Book for 10 May 1941 shows that Sergeant Bauman took off in Hurricane serial L9202 at 21.35 hours on a convoy patrol, landing back at Aldergrove at 22.40 hours.[22] He could not have been anywhere near Hess's aircraft in that period, for the latter was still over the North Sea when Bauman would have had to head back to base. There is no mention of Srom flying on that day, but even if there is a fault in the records, it should be pointed out that the Hurricanes of 245 Squadron were never used as nightfighters. As regards Squadron Leader J.W.C. Simpson, he had served six months as commanding officer of 245 Squadron at the time he was relieved, and this move had no connection with Rudolf Hess.

## HESS'S MESSERSCHMITT WAS PURSUED BY OTHER RAF FIGHTERS

When the news of Hess's arrival became known, other RAF fighter pilots who flew operationally on defensive duties in Scotland on 10 May 1941 assumed they had been sent up to shoot down his Messerschmitt. However, examination of the circumstances in official records verify that they were mistaken, albeit understandably.

There is a difficulty relating to research into such beliefs, for the Operations Records Book (ORBs) of RAF squadrons in the early years of the Second World War are often incomplete. It was one of the functions of hard-pressed squadron adjutants and their small staffs to enter these war diaries, but the work was sometimes regarded as an unnecessary and irksome interruption to the prosecution of the war. The duty was sometimes delegated to a pilot who was grounded temporarily by injury or illness, but such a person could not remain in the orderly room for twenty-four hours a day. Thus there can be omissions in the records. For instance, during the Battle of Britain entries in squadron ORBs which concern casualties are sometimes missing. Some of the operational flights made in early 1941 by one of the authors of this book are not included, although they are entered in his Flying Log Book, signed and countersigned. Details and times of the two Spitfires on patrol when Hess neared Northumberland are not included in the ORB of 72 Squadron, even though their presence is entered in the records of RAF Ouston, the sector commanding RAF Acklington.[23]

One of those who believed he could have shot down Hess was a celebrated New Zealander in the RAF, Flight Lieutenant (later Group Captain) Al Deere, who was serving with the Spitfires of 602 (City of Glasgow) Squadron at Ayr. He had already been credited with shooting down twenty-two enemy aircraft in the Battle of Britain and had become a household name during the war. He later said, 'An Me110 unescorted was a wonderful target. With Hess aboard it was probably the prize fighter-pilot target of the war.'[24]

An examination of the Operations Record Book discloses that there were eight sorties by Spitfires of 602 Squadron on 10 May 1941, the fighters operating in pairs. Flight Lieutenant Deere led the last pair, which took off at 16.35 hours, landing about an hour later.[25] During these daylight hours there was normal German reconnaissance activity. An RAF intelligence report for 10 May includes the following:

> Daylight activity consisted of reconnaissance fighter patrols, fighter sweeps and two minor attacks on land. Bomber reconnaissance aircraft operated from Trondheim, off Orkneys and east coast of Scotland, over North Sea, off East Anglia, over approaches to Bristol Channel and inland over South-west England, Northern Ireland and Scotland. Five aircraft of *KG40* carried out long-range offensive reconnaissance, three of them operating from Norway and one from Bordeaux.[26]

It is obvious that Al Deere was one of the pilots scrambled to deal with these earlier intruders, and made a genuine error when he heard later that Hess had parachuted out over his operational area, not realizing that this had occurred more than four hours after he had landed in his Spitfire. One can be certain that he and his Spitfire would not have been sent up as a nightfighter, for the squadron were not employed on such duties.

A similar assumption was made by another Battle of Britain pilot, Wing Commander F.M. (Hiram) Smith, who wrote a letter which appeared in *The Sunday Telegraph* on 26 May 1991 and including the following:

> I was CO of No 603 Squadron stationed at Drem in East Lothian at the time. . . . A section of two Spitfires, led by Flight Lieutenant G.K. Gilroy DFC (now Group Captain DSO, DFC) was scrambled to intercept Hess's Me110. It was approaching dusk and there was low cloud, which provided cover. In the prevailing conditions, it was not surprising that Hess evaded detection, but had he been intercepted there is little doubt that he would have been shot down, and no instruction was given to prevent this happening.

There are no entries in the records of 603 Squadron, Turnhouse or Drem to substantiate the scrambling of these two Spitfires, but there may have been omissions in the Operations Record Book. However, it is apparent that the Spitfires of this squadron were not in a position to attack Hess's Messerschmitt. The RAF intelligence report for the day continues with:

> At about 22.30 hours two raids were plotted off the Farne Islands and one of these which flew to the Firth of Clyde and Kilmarnock before returning east on a course south of Glasgow was reported shot down.

The 'two raids' were probably those of Hess's single aircraft, which was also the one 'shot down'. The two Spitfires of 603 Squadron were probably sent up to protect Edinburgh against a potential enemy intruder, in weather which was far more overcast there than over the coast of Northumberland. There is no mention of these two fighters in either the Duke of Hamilton's report or the RAF's official investigation into the circumstances of 'Raid 42'. The squadron did not take part in the pursuit of

Hess, although it is certain that the pilots were ready to shoot down any intruders and had not received orders to refrain from doing so.

## THE LUFTWAFFE'S ATTACK ON LONDON WAS A DIVERSION FOR HESS'S FLIGHT

This is a proposition put forward by authors to support their belief that Hess made his flight with the knowledge of Hitler and connivance of Goering. It is implied by the author Peter Padfield who states 'the massed air attacks on London that night were not coincidence'.[27]

It is true that there was a heavy air raid on London during the night of 10/11 May 1941. *Luftflotten* 2 and 3 despatched 520 bombers to the capital and these dropped over 700 tonnes, including many incendiaries. Bombs fell throughout the capital and among the historic buildings damaged were Westminster Abbey, the British Museum, the Houses of Parliament, the Law Courts, the Public Record Office and the Mansion House. Fires were started on both sides of the Thames and some of these joined up to produce huge conflagrations which stretched the emergency forces to the limit. The number of casualties was high, estimated as more than 1,000 killed and 2,000 injured. It was claimed that 33 German raiders were shot down but German figures indicate that only 10 failed to return.[28]

This would have been a very impressive diversion for Hess's flight but it is perfectly clear from the official records that there was no connection. Hess crossed the English coast 300 miles to the north of London at 22.23 hours and finally baled out over Eaglesham at 23.09 hours. There was no air raid alert at London until 23.02 hours, 39 minutes *after* Hess crossed the coast.[29] The bombing of London was indeed serious, and the capital still bears

some of the scars today. But the suggestion that it was a
diversion for Hess's flight has no substance whatsoever.

## IT WAS NOT HESS WHO FLEW TO SCOTLAND BUT AN IMPOSTER

This bizarre theory appeared in a book written by a former
Army surgeon, Hugh Thomas, and published in 1979.[30]
Thomas had attended Hess in Spandau prison during
September 1973 but failed to notice evidence on his body
of the bullet wounds sustained in Romania in the First
World War. In his second book on this subject, he stated:
'The real Hess bore major scars on his chest and back as a
result of his First World War wounds. The man in
Spandau bore none.'[31] This was the primary evidence on
which he based his theory that an imposter flew to Britain
on 10 May 1941, while the real Hess was murdered.

His theory was accompanied by many additional
assertions about the circumstances of Hess's flight
which are demonstrably wrong. For instance, he states
that Hess took off from Augsburg-Haunstetten in a
Messerschmitt Bf110 coded NJ+C11, which was shot
down, probably by a Messerschmitt Bf109, and replaced
by NJ+OQ with an imposter at the controls. But in fact
the code NJ+C11 never existed, in either civil or
military German registrations.

Another assertion is quite extraordinary, for he states
that the code on the side of the aircraft in the Imperial
War Museum is NJ+OQ, the NJ standing for
*Nachtjagdgeschwader* as part of a nightfighter unit code. In
fact, the German nightfighter units never used the code
letters NJ. But above all it is perfectly clear from an
examination of the fuselage in the Imperial War Museum
that the code is VJ+OQ. The letters are about 18 inches
(45.72 cm) high and it is very difficult to understand how

anyone could possibly mistake them. They are the same as those written in Helmut Kaden's log book, as shown in Appendix D of this book.

Another assertion concerns the range of the Messerschmitt Bf110. Thomas states that this was about 850 miles (1,368 km) with internal tanks or 1,200 miles (1,932 km) if it carried the huge drop-tanks each containing 198 gallons (900 litres), whereas the track from Augsburg to Eaglesham, as drawn on the map, was 1,300 miles (2,093 km). His assessment of the performance of the machine is quite incorrect, as can be seen from the calculations based on official figures, shown in Appendix G of this book.

There is plenty of evidence which verifies that the pilot who flew to Scotland on 10 May 1941 was truly Rudolf Hess. He was positively identified by Sir Ivone Kirkpatrick, the Foreign Office expert on Germany, who knew him well. Moreover, Hess recognized Kirkpatrick. While in Britain, Hess wrote to all his family and friends on numerous occasions, his letters containing personal details which only he could have known. His handwriting was identical with that of his letters written pre-war, as can be seen from the examples in Appendices B and H of this book. Nobody at his trial at Nuremberg had any doubts about his identity, nor did his family during their visits to Spandau prison. Moreover a study of photographs taken of Hess before and after his flight to Scotland reveals the same physiognomy – mouth, ears, nose, chin, bushy eyebrows and staring eyes.

With regard to medical evidence, Hess's records show that the bullet wound received while fighting in Romania on 23 July 1917 resulted in a 'pea-sized' entry hole in his chest and a 'cherry stone-sized' exit hole in his back, below the shoulder blade.[32] Professor Bernard Knight, the eminent forensic pathologist, responded in writing on 14 April 1988 to a request from one of the authors of this book for an opinion on whether such scars would remain visible. His letter included the following:

> In forensic pathology there is a wise adage 'Never say never, never say always', and therefore I would hesitate to say that a bullet scar must always be visible or palpable, though I would say that it must always be detectable on a microscopic scale, assuming that one knew where to look.[33]

The question of these tiny scars was also raised with Hess by a Protestant pastor, Charles Gabel, who attended him in Spandau prison. In his book entitled *Conversations Interdites avec Rudolf Hess*, Gabel wrote:

> I told him what had been written in the newspapers about Thomas's book. Hess laughed heartily and told me that two British doctors, the director of the military hospital and a surgeon, had visited him to have a look at these famous scars, which they found, although they were not very visible. . . . There remained only two small scars on the outside, according to him.[34]

A similar comment was reported in the German magazine *Der Spiegel* of 21 May 1979. According to this issue, Hess responded to his wife Ilse when she queried the existence of the wound on his chest: 'You see, the scar is still there, don't worry. It has grown smaller, but it is still there.'

It is true that the medical team which carried out the post-mortem on Hess after his death on 17 August 1987 did not report the existence of these small scars. However, they did report on other wounds:

> No fractures were detected in either forearm, hand, or right humerus (upper arm), while the left humerus

(upper arm) revealed two radio-opaque foreign bodies near the mid to upper shaft suggestive of an old gun-shot wound.[35]

These are consistent with the wounds Hess received on the Western Front. As related in Chapter One, he was hit in the left hand and upper arm on 12 June 1916, and then in the same area of the body on 24 July 1917.

Quite apart from the true identity of Hess, there is the overriding question of why any alleged double would accept imprisonment for life without disclosing his true identity. This is a matter which Hugh Thomas does not explain. Perhaps the most astonishing aspect of his theory is that it has been given credence by some of his readers.

## HESS WAS MURDERED BY THE BRITISH IN SPANDAU

This is another proposition put forward by the author Hugh Thomas, in his second book on the subject of Hess. Still maintaining that the prisoner in Spandau was an imposter, he contends that he was too infirm to have looped a wire round his neck and committed suicide. He believes that the prisoner was beginning to talk loosely about matters which caused the British authorities some alarm. He also finds it amazing that the pathologist chosen to make the post-mortem examination of the body, Professor J.M. Cameron, had not read his first book, which he regarded as 'indispensable reading for anyone with a medical interest in the case'. He comments on the fact that the post-mortem does not record the bullet wounds on chest and back which Hess sustained in Romania, and points out that in another post-mortem carried out by Professor W. Spann of Munich University on 21 August at the request of Hess's son, these wounds are not recorded.

Thomas finds the marks recorded by Professor Spann

round the throat consistent with throttling, and states that they could not possibly have been made by suicide. Thus the prisoner was murdered, not by one of the 'gentle warders', or one of the guards who went everywhere in pairs, but by an intruder. He continues by asserting that the only party to gain from the prisoner's death is the British Government, since it had been covering up the truth about him since 1941. He states that both Professor Spann and Wolf Rüdiger Hess agree with his belief about murder, although the latter is still sure that the dead man was his father. He ends his book by asserting that the cover-up of the true identity of the prisoner by the British Government is a disgraceful crime and demands that the evidence be released.[36]

Since Thomas's last book was published, masses of official documents relating to Hess have been released. All the evidence points to the truth – that the pilot who flew to Scotland on 10 May 1941 was without doubt Rudolf Hess and not an imposter. Thus there was no reason for the British Government to murder Hess in Spandau and indeed many prominent politicians had been campaigning for his release.

Two parts of the additional evidence produced by Hugh Thomas in his second book are easily refuted. He states that the post-mortem revealed that the corpse measured a height of 5 foot 9 inches (1.75 metres), whereas Hess had been about 6 feet 1 inch (1.85 metres) in his youth and could not have withered so much in his old age. This is not true. Hess's medical records of the First World War gave his height at 5 feet 10 inches (1.77 metres) not 6 feet 1 inch (1.85 metres). A reduction of 2 cm in height as a result of stooping in old age is perfectly normal. Thomas includes in his book an X-ray of the torso of Prisoner No. 7 in the British Military Hospital and points out that this showed no sign of the 'massive' bullet wound which Hess sustained in Romania in the First World War. But, according to radiologists, the wound from a bullet which passes through the soft tissues of a body and does not strike a bone, such as that described in detail in Hess's medical records, would certainly not be 'massive'.

With regard to the assertion that the prisoner was murdered, one has to compare Hugh Thomas's opinion that the marks on the neck indicated throttling with the statement of Professor J.M. Cameron, the pathologist who carried out the post-mortem and examined the corpse. Cameron gave the cause of death as asphyxia, compression of the neck, and suspension – i.e. suicide by hanging. One also has to consider whether the verdict of suicide issued by the Four Powers – Britain, France, Russia and the USA – was the result of a conspiracy to conceal the truth, and ask why these officials would have connived for such a purpose. Moreover, one has to ask whether the British Government would have initiated or at least sanctioned the most serious criminal act, that of murder, as suggested by a former officer of the Crown. Those responsible would have been liable under the full force of the law.

There was some support for the murder theory made in a BBC2 *Newsnight* programme on 28 February 1989. One of the witnesses was the Tunisian medical orderly Abdallah Melaouhi, who gave evidence based on his arrival in the 'small summer house' where Hess was found with the cord around his neck. In fact, this was a metal Portakabin, fitted with a heater, where the prisoner could sit and read or doze in comfort. Melaouhi alleged that he had been delayed by the guards, that the furniture had been thrown about as if there had been a struggle in which Hess had attempted to defend himself, that there was no cord around Hess's neck, that the extension cord on the lamp was still in place, that there were two strange men in American uniforms present, and that Hess was so debilitated and arthritic that he could not even tie his own shoelaces, let alone knot a cord round his neck.

By far the most rational replies to these statements come from Lieutenant-Colonel Tony Le Tissier, who was the British Governor of Spandau prison. He points out that the only delay in Melaouhi's arrival was caused by the difficulty in locating him, eventually in the Mess, and even then his time of booking in at the main gate shows that there was little delay before he arrived. There were four reading lamps in the Portakabin and thus more than one cord. The two men in American uniform were medics who had been called to assist in resuscitation, and in fact continued to do so with Melaouhi himself. The furniture had been pushed aside in their previous attempts. With regard to Hess's medical condition, Melaouhi supervised him on an exercise bicycle every morning. Hess wore a truss and probably found bending to tie up his shoelaces difficult, but he could certainly write legibly and thus tie a knot.[37]

Another person who was interviewed on the *Newsnight* programme was Professor Spann, who had carried out the second autopsy on Hess. He stated that the marks on the body did not tally with the normal evidence of people who had been hanged. However, Tony Le Tissier points out that there was no suspension of the body from a noose with the feet off the floor, as is the usual method when people commit suicide by hanging. Hess had removed his outer garments, looped the cord around his neck and slumped to the floor with his legs splayed out in front of him.[38]

Nevertheless, Wolf Rüdiger Hess remains convinced that his father was murdered by the British Government, on the grounds that in 1987 there were signs that the Soviets were likely to agree to release him and that he would disclose certain facts contained in British files not due for release until the year 2017. In April 1995, Wolf Rüdiger submitted evidence to the British Registrar and applied for the wording on his father's death certificate to be changed from 'asphyxiation caused by compression of the neck due to hanging' to 'asphyxiation caused by compression of the neck due to throttling'. A reply was received stating that 'The subject has been studied and it was found that the Services Registering Officer in Germany did not have the authority to register Mr Hess's death. The registration was therefore made in error and the entry relating to Mr Hess has been cancelled.'

This chapter describes only some of the theories which have been put forward after Rudolf Hess's flight to Scotland on 10 May 1941. Doubtless some of the theoreticians genuinely believe in their propositions, although among them are some authors who dismiss facts that are perfectly clear to impartial researchers. Others are opportunists who are aware that there is a public appetite for conspiracy theories and that these are encouraged by certain sections of the media. One matter is certain, however. The flight of Rudolf Hess will continue to intrigue historians for many years to come.

# Notes

## 1. Student, Soldier and Aviator

1. Hess, Ilse. *Ein Schicksal in Briefen*, p. 241.
2. Ibid, p. 493.
3. Ibid, p. 243.
4. Gavrilo Princip, born on 30 June 1894 in Montenegro, was brought to trial and afterwards incarcerated in Theresienstadt prison in Bohemia. He died of tuberculosis of the osseous system on 28 April 1918.
5. BayHStA. Abt.IV Kriegsarchiv.
6. Ibid.
7. Ibid.
8. Ibid.
9. According to the Romanian General Paul Sharp, the battle around the Ungüreana was of such little importance that it was not mentioned in Romanian documents of the period.
10. BayHStA. Abt.VI Kriegsarchiv.
11. Hess, Ilse. *Ein Schicksal in Briefen*, p. 32.
12. Ibid, p. 251.
13. BayHStA. Abt.VI Kriegsarchiv.

## 2. Politician and Aviator

1. Public Record Office, *WO 208/4471*.
2. Hess, Ilse. *Ein Schicksal in Briefen*, p. 18.
3. Ibid, p. 24.
4. Franz-Willing, Georg. *Ursprung der Hitlerbewegung 1919–1922*, p. 215.
5. Snyder, Dr Louis L. *Encyclopedia of the Third Reich*, p. 310.
6. Ibid, p. 20.
7. Toland, John. *Adolf Hitler, Het Einde van een Mythe*, p. 189.
8. Ibid, p. 191.
9. Public Record Office, *WO 208/4471*.
10. Hess, Ilse. *Ein Schicksal in Briefen*, p. 97.
11. Van Ishoven, Armand. *Udet-Biographie*, p. 210.
12. Haus Wachefeld was renovated three times and

eventually renamed as the well-known 'Berghof'.

13. This aircraft was destroyed in March 1932, in the hands of a new owner, from unrecorded causes.

14. Irving, David. *Hess: The Missing Years 1941–1945*, pp. 30–1.

15. Van Ishoven, Armand. *Messerschmitt Der Konstrukteur und Seine Flugzeuge*, p. 111.

16. Public Record Office, *WO 208/4471*.

17. Douglas-Hamilton, James. *Motive for a Mission*, p. 40.

18. Ibid, pp. 37–9.

19. Toland, John. *Adolf Hitler, Het Einde van een Mythe*, p. 391.

20. *Luftwelt*, Bdl, Nr 6, 22 March 1934, p. 86 (Van Ishoven Archives).

21. Orlovius-Schulz. *Die Deutsche Luftfahrt – Jahrbuch 1936*, pp. 183–5 (Van Ishoven Archives).

22. Van Ishoven, Armand. *Messerschmitt Aircraft Designer*, p. 80.

23. Padfield, Peter. *Hess: Flight for the Führer*, p. 56.

24. Snyder, Dr Louis L. *Encyclopedia of the Third Reich*, p. 110.

25. Herschel Grynszpan, born in Hannover in 1921, was charged with murder in Paris and sent to Germany after the surrender of France, where he disappeared.

26. Irving, David. *Rudolf Hess – ein gescheiterter Friedensbote?*, p. 51.

*3. Preparations for the Flight*

1. Public Record Office, *FO 800/317*.

2. Ibid.

3. Douglas-Hamilton, James. *The Truth about Rudolf Hess*, p. 119.

4. Ibid, p. 66.

5. Ibid, pp. 125–33.

6. Van Ishoven, Armand. *Udet-Biographie*, p. 393.

7. Vann, Frank. *Willy Messerschmitt*, pp. 65–7.

8. The prototype of the Bf110, V-1 works number 868, registration D-AHOA, first flew on 12 May 1936, with chief test pilot Dr Ing Hermann Wurster at the controls (Van Ishoven Archives).

9. Freeman, Roger A. *The Mighty Eighth War Diary*, pp. 188 and 219.

10. Letter from Helmut Kaden, 18 July 1989 (Van Acker Archives).

11. *C-Amts-Monatsmeldung* (Technical Department

Monthly Report) for April
1941. (National Archives,
Washington D.C., T-177,
Roll 19, RLM 226.)

12. Helmut Kaden, Flight
Log Books (Van Acker
Archives).

13. Public Record Office,
*INF 1/912*.

14. Padfield, Peter. *Hess:
Flight for the Führer*,
p. 261.

15. Irving, David. *Hess: The
Missing Years*, p. 97.

16. Letter from Helmut
Kaden, 18 July 1989, p. 1
(Van Acker Archives).

17. Ibid, p. 2.

18. Ibid, p. 3.

19. The Beerberg has a
height of 982 metres and
the Inschberg of 916
metres.

20. Leasor, James. *Rudolf
Hess: The Uninvited
Envoy*, pp. 73–81.

21. Irving, David. *Rudolf
Hess – ein gescheiterter
Friedenbote?*, p. 102.

22. Hess, Ilse. *Ein Schicksal
in Briefen*, p. 78.

23. This vast and partly
subterranean complex
was built before 1936. It
also housed the
*Generalstab der Luftwaffe*
(General Staff of the Air
Force). In the last stages
of the war, it housed the
*Oberkommando der
Wehrmacht* OKW (Armed
Forces of the General
Staff).

24. Letter from Dr 'F.S.', 10
July 1993 (Van Acker
Archives). Our informant
did not wish to be
identified to the general
public, to avoid
unwelcome attention.
Although he died on 1
May 1995, the authors
must keep their promise.

25. Public Record Office, *FO
1093/8*.

26. Ibid, *FO 1093/10*.

27. Ibid, *WO 208/4471*.

28. Weather map for
Saturday 10 May 1941,
courtesy Deutscher
Wetterdienst-
Seewetteramt, Hamburg.

29. Hess, Ilse. *Ein Schicksal
in Briefen*, p. 68.

30. Alfred Rosenberg was
born in Estonia on 12
January 1893, of an
Estonian mother and a
Lithuanian father. He
was brought to trial at
Nuremberg after the war,
found guilty on all four
counts and hanged.

31. Padfield, Peter. *Hess:
Flight for the Führer*,
p. 193.

32. Ibid, p. 219.

33. Hinsley, F.H. et al. *British

*Intelligence in the Second World War*, volume 1, p. 433.

34. Ibid, p. 479.

35. Hess, Ilse. *Ein Schicksal in Briefen*, p. 69.

36. Ibid, p. 70.

37. Letter from Helmut Kaden, 8 November 1989, p. 2 (Van Acker Archives).

38. Hess, Ilse. *Ein Schicksal in Briefen*, p. 70.

39. Padfield, Peter. *Hess: Flight for the Führer*, p. 194.

40. Ibid, pp. 194–5.

41. It is evident from the extracts from Helmut Kaden's logbooks that test flying took place on Saturdays and Sundays as well as on other days of the week.

42. The German colloquial expression for good luck.

43. There was a tendency to tail wheel shimmying in the earlier Bf110s. In August 1940 tests were carried out on Bf110D fighter-bombers at the *Technische Hochschule* (Technical University) in Stuttgart-Untertürkheim with regard to the intensity of shimmying in relation to the inclination of the shock absorber strut. Shimmying was reduced to a minimum at a certain angle but shock absorption properties declined. A solution was achieved by a compromise between the two factors. (NASM Archives Division, ref: R2963 F199). In May 1941 test pilot Kühnle carried out a test flight with a Bf110E, works number 3850, radio code NM+IX. He reported 'At take-off and landing the tail wheel did not shimmy. Even when the landing flaps were retracted and thus the speed was higher, shimmy did not occur.' (NASM Archives Division, ref: R2497 F698).

44. Local times were identical in Britain and Germany in this period of the war. British Double Summer Time (two hours in advance of Greenwich Mean Time) began at 02.00 hours on 4 May 1941. German Summer Time (also two hours in advance of Greenwich Mean Time) began at 02.00 hours on 1 April 1940 and continued until 02.00 hours on 2 November 1942.

## 4. The Flight

1. Archives Services Manager, Meteorological Office, Bracknell.
2. Public Record Office, *FO 1093/1*.
3. Ibid.
4. Ibid.
5. Ibid.
6. Galland, Adolf. *The First and the Last*, pp. 108–9.
7. Hess, Ilse. *Ein Schicksal in Briefen*, p. 211.
8. Correspondence with Lennoxlove, October/November 1995 (Nesbit Archives).
9. Public Record Office, *FO 1093/1*.
10. Ashbee, Felicity. *The Thunderstorm that was Hess*.
11. Public Record Office, *AIR 28/624*.
12. Public Record Office, *AIR 27/624*.
13. He had been slightly wounded in the left leg and wrist during a combat with Bf109s on 1 September 1940, when flying Spitfire I serial L1056 of 72 Squadron from Croydon in Surrey. In spite of his wounds, he had made a skilful belly landing at West Malling in Kent, and returned to his squadron after hospital treatment.
14. Discussions with Flight Lieutenant Maurice A. Pocock, 25 July 1989.
15. Public Record Office, *FO 1093/1*.
16. Ibid.
17. Wood, Derek. *Attack Warning Red*, p. 1.
18. Ibid, p. 2.
19. Correspondence with Wing Commander C.H. Maclean, September/October 1993.
20. Public Record Office, *AIR 27/969*.
21. Public Record Office, *FO 1093/1*.
22. Squadron Leader William A. Cuddie was killed in action on 3 October 1943 while leading an attack by Beaufighters of 46 Squadron from Lakatamia in Cyprus against German forces in the island of Cos.
23. Public Record Office, *FO 1093/1*.
24. Wood, Derek. *Attack Warning Red*, p. 3.

## 5. The Next Ten Days

1. Public Record Office, *FO 1093/1*.
2. Leasor, James. *Rudolf Hess: The Uninvited Envoy*, p. 25.

3. Ibid, p. 27.
4. Hess, Ilse. *Prisoner of Peace*, p. 36.
5. Leasor, James. *Rudolf Hess: The Uninvited Envoy*, p. 30.
6. Public Record Office, *WO 190/3288A*.
7. Hess, Ilse. *Prisoner of Peace*, p. 36.
8. Public Record Office, *WO 190/3288A*.
9. Ibid, *AIR 16/1266*.
10. Ibid.
11. Ibid, *AIR 28/861*.
12. Ibid, *AIR 27/1106*.
13. Ibid, *PREM 3/219/7*.
14. Correspondence with Wing Commander C.H. Maclean, September/ October 1993 (Nesbit Archives).
15. Public Record Office, *INF 1/912*.
16. Ibid, *PREM 2/219/7*.
17. Ibid, *INF 1/912*.
18. Ibid, *AIR 16/519*.
19. Colville, Sir John. *The Fringes of Power*, pp. 386–9.
20. Letter from Helmut Kaden, 31 January 1991 (Van Acker Archives).
21. Speer, Albert. *Inside the Third Reich*, p. 174.
22. Public Record Office, *INF 1/912*.
23. Ibid, *FO 1093/1*.
24. Taylor, Fred. *The Goebbels Diaries 1939–41*, p. 363.
25. Public Record Office, *INF 1/912*.
26. Ibid, *WO 199/3288B*.
27. This X-ray no longer exists. According to the radiologist Michael Fowler, the small calcified area may have been the result of a minor attack of tuberculosis in childhood. (Interview, 27 September 1996).
28. Public Record Office, *KV 2/37*.
29. Ibid, *WO 199/3288B*.
30. *Records from the Tower of London*, p. 136.

*6. Hess's Messerschmitt*

1. Public Record Office, *AIR 29/1019*.
2. Ibid, *PREM 3/219/7*.
3. Nesbit, Roy. *Hess's Last Flight*.
4. Letter dated 4 September 1991 (Van Acker Archives).
5. Detailed drawings, together with the parts list, of the *Schlauchboot-Einbau* (built-in dinghy release) are available for the Bf110D. These were the same as for the Bf110E (C. Vanhee Archives).
6. There were two other variants of the Bf110

which had an extended tail section, the Bf110D-0 and the Bf110-0B, but these were equipped with DB601A engines.

7. Fresh air for the pilot's heater was provided from a rectangular opening in the nose, between the muzzles of the machine-guns. Detailed drawings are available showing some of the resemblances and differences between the Bf110D and the Bf110E (C. Vanhee Archives).

8. *Lieferplan Nr 17c* (Delivery Programme No. 17c), 3 July 1940. *Soll-u. 1st – Ablieferung der Flugzeuge* (estimated and actual supply of aircraft), 19 April 1940. (National Archives, Washington D.C., T-177, Roll 19, RLM 233).

9. Wood, Derek. *Attack Warning Red*, p. 4.

10. Hess, Ilse. *Prisoner of Peace*, p. 138.

11. *Bf110 mit 2 motoren DB601A oder DB601N (KBA-F1.)* (NASM Archives Division, Washington D.C., Reel 8168, I.P. No. 2746.)

12. Public Record Office, *HO 199/305*.

### 7. *Prisoner for Life*

1. Public Record Office, *PREM 3/219/7*.
2. Ibid, *FO 1093/11*.
3. Ibid, *WO 166/1260*.
4. Masterman, J.C. *The Double-Cross System*.
5. Public Record Office, *WO 166/2293*.
6. Ibid, *WO 166/1260*.
7. Ibid, *HO 201/9*.
8. *Luton News*, 29 May 1941.
9. *Luton at War*, 1947, reprinted by Home Counties Newspapers in 1982.
10. Interview with author, 16 October 1996.
11. Farago, Ladislas. *The Game of the Foxes*, pp. 280 and 328.
12. Stahl, P.W. *KG200: The True Story*, pp. 51 and 185.
13. Public Record Office, *HO 324/1*.
14. After The Battle, number 11. *German Spies in Britain*, pp. 28–9.
15. Taylor, Fred. *The Goebbels Diaries 1939–41*, p. 424.
16. Public Record Office, *FO 1093/8*.
17. Public Record Office, *PREM 3/219/7*.
18. Ibid, *FO 1093/1*.
19. Ibid.
20. Ibid.
21. Ibid, *FO 1093/14*.

22. Ibid, *FO 1093/10*.
23. Ibid, *PREM 3/219/2*.
24. Ibid, *FO 1093/2*.
25. Ibid, *FO 1093/14*.
26. Ibid, *PREM 3/219/7*.
27. Ibid, *FO 1093/17*.
28. Ibid, *HS 6/623*.
29. Ibid.
30. Rees, J.R. *The Case of Rudolf Hess*, pp. 74 and 130.
31. Le Tissier, Tony. *Berlin Then and Now*, pp. 345–7.
32. *Gazet van Antwerpen*, 7 September 1987.
33. Le Tissier, Tony. *Farewell to Spandau*, pp. 46–50.
34. Ibid, pp. 51–2.
35. Churchill, Winston. *History of the Second World War*, volume III, p. 49.

## 8. Some of the Myths

1. Public Record Office, *KV 2/38*.
2. *The Times*, 19 February 1942.
3. Werth, Alexander. *Rusland in Oorlog – 1941–1945*, pp. 237–8.
4. Public Record Office, *PREM 3/434/7*.
5. *New York Times*, 8 June 1991.
6. *The Times, Obituary Herr Rudolf Hess*, 18 August 1987.
7. *Svenska Dagbladet*, 13 May 1941.
8. Public Record Office, press release dated 27 January 1999.
9. Ibid, *KV 2/38*.
10. Harris, John & Trow, M.J. *Hess: The British Conspiracy*, p. 11.
11. Ibid, p. 21.
12. de Wijn, Jan Willem, *Landde Hess op Schiphol?*, pp. 2 and 5.
13. Ibid, pp. 3 and 5.
14. Zwanenburg, Gerrit J. *En Nooit Was Het Stil . . .*, pp. 195–6.
15. *Svenska Dagbladet*, 23 May 1941.
16. Padfield, Peter. *Hess: Flight for the Führer*, pp. 195–6.
17. Roba, Jean-Louis. *Reinhard Heydrich et la Luftwaffe*, pp. 7–9.
18. Nesbit Archives.
19. Ibid.
20. Costello, John. *Ten Days That Saved The West*, pp. 5–6.
21. Ibid, p. 5.
22. Public Record Office, *AIR 27/1481*.
23. Ibid, *AIR 28/624*.
24. *The Daily Telegraph, Obituary Air Cdre Al Deere*, 23 September 1995.
25. Public Record Office, *AIR 27/2075*.

26. Ibid, *AIR 22/116*.
27. Padfield, Peter. *Hess: Flight for the Führer*, p. 259.
28. Ramsey, Winston. *The Blitz Then and Now*, volume two, pp. 608–18.
29. Public Record Office, *WO 166/1294*.
30. Thomas, Hugh. *The Murder of Rudolf Hess*, p. 26.
31. Thomas, Hugh. *Hess: a Tale of Two Murders*, p. 167.
32. BayHStA. Abt.IV Kriegsarchiv.
33. Nesbit Archives.
34. Gabel, Charles. *Conversations Interdites avec Rudolf Hess*, p. 73.
35. Autopsy Report on Allied Prisoner No. 7, p. 2.
36. Thomas, Hugh. *Hess: a Tale of Two Murders*, pp. 172–95.
37. Le Tissier, Tony. *Farewell to Spandau*, pp. 101–4.
38. Ibid, pp. 75 and 104.

# Transcript of notice issued by Rudolf Hess on 10 November 1938

DER STELLVERTRETER DES FÜHRERS
AN ALLE GAULEITUNGEN ZUR SOFORTIGEN
VERANLASSUNG!

Anordnung Nr 174/38                    München, den 10. November 1938

Auf ausdrücklichen Befehl allerhöchster Stelle dürfen Brandlegungen an jüdischen Geschäften oder dergleichen auf gar keinen Fall und under gar keinen Umständen erfolgen.

Translation:

THE DEPUTY FUHRER
IMMEDIATE RECOMMENDATION TO ALL
PROVINCIAL GOVERNORS!

ORDINANCE No. 174/38                    Munich,    10 November 1938

On explicit order from the highest level, no incendiary actions against Jewish businesses or the like are to take place, for any reasons or on any account.

(German text reproduced by courtesy of the publishers Leopold Stocker Verlag of Graz, taken from the book *Rudolf Hess – Ein Gescheiterter Friedensbote?* by David Irving, BDC Akte, Ordner, 240/1.)

# Letter written by Rudolf Hess to his wife on 4 November 1940

Translation:

Berlin, 4.11.40

My dear,

I firmly believe that from the flight I am about to make one of these days, I will return and the flight will be crowned with success. However, if not, the goal I have set myself will have been worth the supreme effort. I know that all of you understand me; you will know that I could not have acted otherwise.

Your,

Rudolf

RUDOLF HESS

MÜNCHEN-HARLACHING
HARTHAUSERSTRASSE 4A

Berlin, 4. 11. 40

Meine Lieben,

ich glaube fest daran, daß ich von dem Flug, den ich nächster Tage antrete, zurückkehre u. daß der Flug von Erfolg gekrönt sein wird. Wenn aber nicht, so war das Ziel, das ich mir stellte, des vollen Einsatzes Wert. Ich weiß, daß Ihr mich kennt: Ihr wißt, ich konnte nicht anders handeln.

Euer Rudolf.

# List of Rudolf Hess's test flights according to various sources

| Date | Details | Flying time | |
|------|---------|-------------|---|
| | | Hrs | Mins |
| ?? Jan 1941 (James Douglas-Hamilton) | Returned owing to bad weather | 4 | – |
| 10 Jan 1941 | Rudder jammed – could not gain height | Not stated | |
| 30 Apl 1941 (Edgar W. Geiss) | Returned owing to bad weather | Not stated | |
| 10 Jan 1941 | None given | 4 | 10 |
| 30 Apl 1941 (Wolf Rüdiger Hess) | Cancelled on Hitler's orders | Cancelled | |
| 10 Jan 1941 (David Irving) | Returned owing to bad weather | 4 | ? |
| 21 Dec 1940 | Loose Very pistol jammed in rudder cables, turned back | 3 | |
| 18 Jan 1941 | Unable to receive signal from Kalundborg radio station | 3 | 30 |
| 30 Apl 1941 (Helmut Kaden) | Cancelled on Hitler's orders | Cancelled | |
| ?? Jan 1941 | Aileron jammed – could not gain height | 4 | 25 |
| Not stated (R. Manvell & H. Fraenkel) | Returned owing to bad weather | Not stated | |

| Date | Details | Flying time |     |
| --- | --- | --- | --- |
|      |         | Hrs | Mins |
| 21 Dec 1940 | No details. Mentions Kaden as source | Not stated | |
| 7 Jan 1941 | Returned owing to bad weather and problems with plane at factory. Mentions Hess as source. | Not stated | |
| 10 Jan 1941 | Hess's first attempt to reach Scotland. Mentions Pintsch as source. | Not stated | |
| 18 Jan 1941 (Peter Padfield) | None given | Not stated | |
| 11 Jan 1941 | Defect in elevator, plane would not climb | – | 30 |
| 08 Mar 1941 (Wulf Schwarzwäller) | Returned owing to bad weather | 1 | 15 |
| ?? Nov 1940 | Mentions Kaden as source | Not stated | |
| ?? Jan 1941 | Ailerons jammed, could not cross mountains | 4 | 30 |
| 29 Jan 1941 | Returned owing to bad weather. Mentions Kaden as source | Not stated | |
| (Hugh Thomas) | | | |

*Note from authors*:
Some of the above are contradictory. We have relied mostly on Helmut Kaden.

# APPENDIX D

# *Section of Pilot's Log Book kept by Flugkapitän a.D. Helmut Kaden*

| Zulassungs- Nr. des Flugzeugs | Führer | Fluggast | Zweck des Fluges | Abflug | | |
|---|---|---|---|---|---|---|
| | | | | Ort | Tag 19 41 | |
| b | c | d | e | f | g | |
| BF 110 | Kaden | – | Kontrollflug | Augsburg | 3/5 | |
| " | " | Major S | | " | 4/5 | |
| " | " | – | Einflug | " | " | |
| " | " | Taugler Noack | Kunstlereiefl. | " | " | |
| " | " | Blümel Kircher | Sp.-flug | " | | |
| " | " | Major S | Kontrollfl. | " | 5/5 | |
| " | " | Taugler Noack | Kunstmnefl. | " | " | |
| " | " | Leitenmeier | Kontrollfl. | " | " | |
| " | " | Blümel Kircher | Sp.-flug | " | 6/5 | |
| " | " | | | " | " | |
| " | " | Luig | Kontrollfl. | " | " | |
| " | " | Störkmann | | " | " | |
| " | " | | " | " | " | |
| " | " | Hörmann | | " | " | |

The chief test pilot for the Messerschmitt Works outlined in his log book the last test flight he made with Rudolf Hess's Bf110 radio code VJ+OQ, on 6 May 1941. He was accompanied on this flight by Josef Blümel, the chief wireless operator for the Messerschmitt Works, who made the final tests on the radio and navigational equipment. Samstag (Saturday) was the day when Hess flew to Scotland, four days later.

Source: The late *Flugkapitän a.D.* Helmut Kaden

| Landung | | | gellog. Zeit | | Auftrag | | Bemerkungen |
| Ort | Tag 1941 | Uhrzeit | h | min | Auftrag- geber | Auftrag Nr. | |
| i | k | l | m | n | o | p | q |
| Aug | 3/5 | 15 12 | | 28 | PN + PB | 113 | |
| " | 4/5 | 9 36 | | 22 | BC+HV | 4055 | |
| " | " | 11 32 | | 27 | BC+HZ | 4164 | |
| " | " | 11 39 | | 40 | BC+HY | 4156 | |
| " | " | 12 51 | | 24 | BC+HY | 4854 | |
| " | 5/5 | 6 36 | | 18 | BC+HU | 4055 | |
| " | " | 14 14 | | 37 | BC+HZ | 4164 | |
| " | " | 15 16 | | 9 | BC+HV | 4156 | |
| " | 6/5 | 16 30 | | 25 | BC+HZ | 4060 | |
| " | " | 11 41 | | 12 | VJ+OQ | 3160 | Hess-Maschine   samstag |
| " | " | 11 59 | | 19 | BC+HF | 4040 | |
| " | " | 12 13 | | 8 | BC+HZ | 4060 | |
| " | " | 14 30 | | 7 | " | 4060 | |
| " | " | 15 06 | | 11 | " | 4160 | |
| | | | | 279 | | | |

# APPENDIX E

# *Verbatim Transcript of Official Report*

*OPERATIONAL RESEARCH SECTION (F.C.)    REPORT NO. 195*
1. The following is the probable history of this track in plan position and height, based on an investigation of recorded R.D.F. information.

## 2. *Plan Position of Raid 42*

*2.1* The aircraft was picked up by R.D.F. Stations at approximately R.2545 and came in almost due west travelling at a speed of approximately 300 m.p.h., as shown by the red line. According to the Operations Room tracing, as shown by the green line, at approximately Q.4535 the track bends northwest and, having circled, makes a landfall off Holy Island as Raid X.42. No Observer Corps track takes over from this track X.42.

*2.2* It will be seen, however, that by continuing the track due westwards from Q.4535, that it connects up with the Observer Corps Raid 42 J. in plan position. The discrepancy in time is accounted for by the time lag of approximately 3 minutes between the true track and the Operations Room track.

*2.3* The filtered track after Q.4535 is not that of Raid 42 but a fighter aircraft despatched to intercept Raid 42. The reason for this is that, after this point Q.4535, very little R.D.F. information was forthcoming on Raid 42 because of its height and position with respect to various stations. Most of the plotting was on the fighters and Raid 42 was continued on this information.

3. *Strength of Raid 42*

*3.1* The strength of Raid 42 was estimated as 1 aircraft by Danby Beacon CH., Bamburgh CH.L. and Creswell CH.L., when these stations were actually plotting on it. Ottercops Moss CH., however, reported it as 3+ aircraft.

*3.2* In view of the discrepancies that occur in counting between R.D.F. stations, it is thought that the Ottercops Moss estimate should be waived in favour of the estimate of the other four stations.

4. *Height of Raid 42*

*4.1* It seems that the aircraft in its course into the coast was either at too low an angle of elevation or unsuitably placed in azimuth for a good '1,000 ft height reading' to be obtained from any CH. station.

*4.2* An investigation of the heights passed, together with the performances of stations on this raid, indicate that the aircraft, when first detected, was approximately 15,000 ft and came down in a shallow dive to approximately 10,000 ft at Q.4535. Presumably this loss of altitude was continued to the coast as a height of 5,000 ft is reported by the Observer Corps on 42 J.

5. *Previous Enemy Activity*

*5.1* Previous enemy activity in this area is confined to a short outgoing track Raid 39 occurring approximately half an hour before Raid 42. This track was plotted by Ottercops Moss CH. alone as 1 aircraft and no height was given on it.

*5.2* No relationship between Raid 42 and Raid 39 or any other track can be found, and in view of the 'sudden' appearance of Raid 42 flying at 300 m.p.h. in the area illuminated by R.D.F., it seems likely that Raid 42 was on a set course when detected.

*O.R.S.4/14/7.*
*JCT/CMS. 18th May 1941*

*Notes by authors:*
1. F.C. = Fighter Command.
2. R.D.F. = Radio Direction Finding.
3. The positions R.2454 and Q.4535 are based on graticule codes which changed from time to time and have now been lost.
4. CH = Chain Home.
5. CH.L. = Chain Home Low (directed at low-flying aircraft).

# Specification of Messerschmitt Bf110E-2/N

**Engines** Two Daimler-Benz DB601/N, twelve-cylinder, inverted-vee (60°), four-stroke, liquid-cooled, injection engines. *Maximum rpm at 4,900 metres*: 2,600. *Maximum power*: 1,175 hp with 2,600 rpm. *Maximum cruising power at 5,100 metres*: 950 hp with 2,300 rpm. *Propeller*: three-bladed, right-hand tractor, adjustable pitch, fully feathering VDM (Vereinigte Deutsche Metalwerke) with diameter of 3.35 metres.

**Fuel Capacity** Four internal tanks in the wings, two of 375 litres and two of 260 litres. When fitted with two drop-tanks (*Rüstsatz* B2) of 900 litres each, total fuel capacity was 3,070 litres of C3 fuel (100 octane).

**Oil Capacity** Two internal oil tanks with a capacity of 35 litres each. Some Bf110s also carried a jettisonable oil tank (*Rüstsatz* B1), containing 75 litres of oil, beneath the fuselage near the wing roots. This oil could be pumped manually into the internal oil tanks, the pump and change-over switch being normally operated by the second crew member.

**Dimensions** *Span*: 16.30 metres. *Length*: 12.10 metres. *Height*: 3.90 metres. *Wing area*: 38.40 metres$^2$.

**Weight** *Empty*: 5,200 kg. *Loaded (normal)*: 6,750 kg.

**Performance** *Maximum speed at sea level*: 473 km/hr. *Maximum speed at 7,000 metres*: 562 km/hr. *Cruising speed at 5,000 metres*: 490 km/hr. *Maximum climb with normal load*: 6,000 metres in 11 minutes. *Service ceiling*: 10,000 metres. *Radius of action with two 900-litre drop-tanks, at cruising speed of 490 km/hr at 5,000 metres*: 2,000 km.

# APPENDIX G

# *Calculation of Hess's Flight on 10 May 1941*

From take-off at Augsburg-Haunstetten at 17.45 hours until parachute landing at Floors Farm at 23.09 hours (CET = BDST)

| | Height *Metres* | Fuel Consumption *Litres* | Speed *Km/Hr* | Time *Hr* | *Min* | Distance *Km* |
|---|---|---|---|---|---|---|
| 1. | 300 | 15 | 210 | 0 | 01 | 1 |
| 2. | 300 | 890 | 450 | 2 | 02 | 758 |
| 3. | 5,000 | 285 | 205 | 0 | 19 | 70 |
| 4. | 5,000 | 840 | 420 | 1 | 36 | 563 |
| 5. | 3,000 | 415 | 445 | 0 | 42 | 310 |
| 6. | 300 or lower | 445 | 405 | 0 | 42 | 248 |
| 7. | 2,000 | 60 | 210 | 0 | 04 | 3 |
| *Totals* | | 2,950 | | 5 | 26 | 1,953 |

| *Summary* | | Time *Hr* | *Min* |
|---|---|---|---|
| 1. | Climbing to 300 metres | | |
| 2. | Over Germany, Holland and North Sea | 2 | 03 |
| 3. | Climbing to 5,000 metres over North Sea | 0 | 19 |
| 4. | Over North Sea with drop-tanks | | |
| 5. | Over North Sea without drop-tanks | 2 | 18 |
| 6. | Over England and Scotland | | |
| 7. | Climbing and baling out | 0 | 46 |
| *Total* | | 5 | 26 |

Note: Calculations are based on the official Luftwaffe document *Flugstrecken Bf110D u. E mit DB01A* [engines] *mit abwerfbaren Behältern* [drop-tanks each with 400 litres], *Bomben 2 2 500 kg* [carrying two 500 kg bombs], adjusted to represent Hess's Bf110E-2/N with DB601N engines and two 900-litre drop-tanks.

# APPENDIX H

# *First page of the letter written by Rudolf Hess to his son, 10–15 June 1941*

This letter was written while Hess was in captivity in Britain. The handwriting may be compared with the letter he wrote to his wife before his flight (Appendix B).

# APPENDIX I

# *Petrol and Oil Transfer System in the Messerschmitt Bf110E*

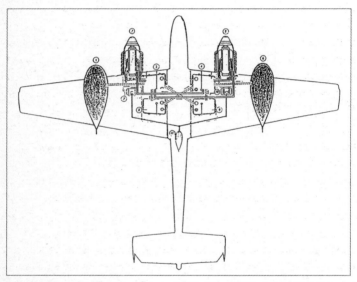

Drawing key:

| | |
|---|---|
| (1) | Port 900-litre jettisonable fuel tank |
| (2) | Port Daimler-Benz DB601/N engine |
| (3) | Port 375-litre main fuel tank |
| (4) | Starboard 375-litre main fuel tank |
| (5) | Starboard Daimler-Benz DB601/N engine |
| (6) | Starboard 900-litre jettisonable fuel tank |
| (7) | Port 35-litre oil tank |
| (8) | Port 260-litre reserve fuel tank |
| (9) | Starboard 260-litre reserve tank |
| (10) | Starboard 35-litre main oil tank |
| (11) | Jettisonable 75-litre oil tank |

Remarks:  - - - - -  fuel transfer from main tanks to engines.
                 = = = =  fuel transfer from drop- or reserve tanks to main tanks.
                 ————  oil transfer from drop-tank to both main oil tanks.

Both engines (2 and 5) were fed solely from the main petrol tanks of 375 litres (3 and 4) inboard of each engine and forward of the single main spar. Each main tank could feed either engine, or both at the same time. The pilot controlled the flow of petrol to the engines from switches in his instrument panel, assisted by warning lights. For each main tank there was a white warning light which came on when the petrol was down to 240 litres.

In the first part of a flight, these main petrol tanks were always replenished by boost pressure from the 900-litre drop-tanks (1 and 6) beneath the wings. This continued until the white warning lights remained on, indicating that the drop-tanks were empty. The pilot then pulled a lever in the floor, to the right of his seat, and jettisoned the drop-tanks. A non-return valve prevented the petrol from flowing out of the disconnected fuel pipes.

After the drop-tanks had been jettisoned, the pilot replenished the main tanks from the reserve tanks of 260 litres (8 and 9) situated aft of the main spar. Petrol was pumped into them until two red lights lit up on the instrument panel, indicating that the reserve tanks were empty and that only the 375 litres in each main tank remained. If flying continued on the main tanks, the white lights came on again when the petrol in each tank was down to 240 litres. The red lights came on again when only 90 litres remained in each main tank.

In addition to the supply of petrol, the crew had to control the supply of oil in the left and right tanks (7 and 10) situated behind each engine. This was replenished from the oil drop-tank (11) below the fuselage. The change-over switch and pump handle were normally installed in the rear compartment on the left side of the second crew member, but it seems that Hess arranged for these to be moved to the pilot's position, which would have presented no difficulty. After a flying time of about one hour, by using the switch and pump handle, 7.5 litres of oil were transferred to each oil tank in the wings. Pumping was discontinued for a very short while after about two minutes, to allow a restrictor to function freely, but could soon be resumed. When the oil tanks were full, the pump handle could no longer be moved. The empty oil drop-tank could be jettisoned only from the rear cockpit.

This procedure was the same for the Messerschmitt Bf110D.

Source: *Bf110 mit 2 motoren DB601A oder DB601N*, Reel 8168, I.P. No. 2746. NASM, Archives Division, Washington D.C.

# Bibliography

Air Historical Branch (RAF). *Interrogation of Professor Willy Messerschmitt by the US Strategic Bombing Survey Team at the end of the War.*

Air Historical Branch (RAF). *18 May 1941. Investigation of Raid 42 on 10th May 1941.*

Ashbee, Felicity. *The Thunderstorm that was Hess.* Sutton: Aeroplane Monthly, October 1987.

Bird, E. *The Loneliest Man in the World.* London: Secker & Warburg, 1974.

Churchill, W. *The Second World War, Vol. III.* London: Cassell, 1950.

Colville, Sir John. *The Fringes of Power.* London: Hodder & Stoughton, 1985.

Costello, John. *Ten Days that Saved the West.* London: Bantam, 1991.

*Der Spiegel*, Germany. 'The Riddle of the VJ+OQ', 21 May 1979.

Deschner, Günther. *Heydrich.* London: Orbis, 1981.

Douglas-Hamilton, James. *The Truth about Rudolf Hess.* Edinburgh: Mainstream, 1993.

Farago, Ladislas. *The Game of the Foxes.* New York: Bantam Books, 1973.

Gabel, C.A. *Conversations Interdites avec Rudolf Hess.* Paris: Plon, 1988.

*Gazet van Antwerpen.* Articles, 7 September 1987, 2 March 1989.

Geiss, Edgar W. *Rudolf Hess – Märtyrer für den Frieden.* Hechthausen: Verlag Edgar W. Geiss, 1988.

Galland, Adolf. *The First and the Last.* London: Methuen, 1955.

Green, W. *Warplanes of the Third Reich.* London: Military Book Society, 1970.

Hamilton, Ian B.M. *The Happy Warrior.* London: Cassell, 1966.

Harris, John & Trow, M.J. *Hess: The British Conspiracy*. London: André Deutsch, 1999.

Hess, Ilse. *Prisoner of Peace*. London: Britons, 1954.

Hess, Ilse. *Ein Schicksal in Briefen*. Leoni am Starnberger See: Druffel-Verlag, 1984.

Hess, Wolf Rüdiger. *My Father Rudolf Hess*. London: W.H. Allen, 1986.

Hess, Wolf Rüdiger. *Mord an Rudolf Hess?* Leoni am Starnberger See: Druffel-Verlag, 1990.

Hinsley, F.H. et al. *British Intelligence in the Second World War, Vol. 1*. London: HMSO, 1979.

Hutton, J.B. *Hess*. London: David Bruce & Watson, 1970.

Huntly, I.D. 'An Observer's Diary'. *Airfix Magazine*, December 1985.

Hydrographic Office, Taunton. *Tidal Stream Atlas: Firth of Clyde and Approaches*, NP 222, Edition 1-1992.

Irving, David. *Hess: The Missing Years 1941–1945*. London: Grafton Books, 1987.

Irving, David. *Rudolf Hess – ein gescheiterter Friedensbote?* Graz: Leopold Stocker Verlag, 1987.

Ishoven, Armand van. *Messerschmitt Aircraft Designer*. London: Gentry Books, 1975.

Ishoven, Armand van. *Messerschmitt – Der Konstrukteur und seine Flugzeuge*. Wien: Paul Neff Verlag, 1975.

Ishoven, Armand von. *Udet-Biographie*. Wien: Paul Neff Verlag, 1977.

Johnstone, Sandy. *Where No Angels Dwell*. London: Jarrolds, 1969.

Law Officers Department. *Trial of Major German War Criminals*. London: HMSO, 1949.

Leasor, J. *Rudolf Hess: The Uninvited Envoy*. London: George Allen & Unwin, 1962.

Le Tissier, Tony. *Berlin Then and Now*. London: After the Battle, 1984.

Le Tissier, Tony. *Farewell to Spandau*. Leatherhead: Ashford, Buchan & Knight, 1994.

Manvell, Roger & Fraenkel, Heinrich. *Hess*. London: McGibbon & Kee, 1971.

Masterman, J.C. *The Double-Cross System*. London: Pimlico, 1995.

Nesbit, Roy. 'Hess's Last Flight'. London: *Aeroplane Monthly*, June 1995.

Paape, A.H. et al. *Handboek van de Tweede Wereldoorlog*. Utrecht/Antwerpen: Het Spectrum, 1980.

Padfield, Peter. *Hess: Flight for the Führer*. London: Weidenfeld & Nicholson, 1991.

Padfield, Peter. *Hess: The Führer's Disciple*. London: Papermac, 1995.

Philby, Kim. *My Secret War*. London: MacGibbon & Kee, 1968.

Ramsay, Winston G. (ed.) *After the Battle*, no. 11, 1976; *After the Battle*, no. 58, 1987.

Ramsay, Winston G. (ed.) *The Blitz Then and Now, Volume Two*. London: After the Battle, 1988.

Rees, J.R. *The Case of Rudolf Hess*. London: Heinemann, 1947.

Richards, D. *Royal Air Force 1939–45*. London: HMSO, 1953.

Shirer, William L. *The Rise and Fall of the Third Reich*. London: Secker & Warburg, 1959.

Speer, Albert. *Inside the Third Reich*. London: Weidenfeld and Nicholson, 1971.

Stahl, P.W. *KG200: The True Story*. London: Jane's, 1981.

*Svenska Dagbladet*, Sweden. Articles, 13, 15 and 23 May 1941.

Taylor, Fred. *The Goebbels Diaries 1939–41*. London: Hamish Hamilton, 1982.

Thomas, Hugh. *The Murder of Rudolf Hess*. London: Hodder & Stoughton, 1979.

Thomas, Hugh. *Hess: A Tale of Two Murders*. London: Hodder & Stoughton, 1988.

Tusa, Ann & Tusa, John. *The Nuremberg Trial*. London: Macmillan Books, 1983.

Vann, Frank. *Willy Messerschmitt – First Full Biography of an Aeronautical Genius*. Sparkford: Patrick Stephens, 1993.

Werth, Alexander. *Rusland in Oorlog 1941–1945*. Amsterdam: Omega Boek B.V., 1979.

West, K.S. *The Captive Luftwaffe*. London: Putnam, 1978.

Wijn, Jan Willem de. 'Landde Hess op Schiphol?' *Schipholland*, 30 April 1991.

Wood, D. *Attack Warning Red*. London: MacDonald & Janes, 1976.

Wright, Ian B. *Investigation Report: The Rudolf Hess Parachute Enigma*. October 1993.

Zwanenburg, Gerrit J. *En Nooit Was Het Stil . . . Deel 1*. Netherlands: DMKlu, undated.


*Imperial War Museum*, London

FD4355/45 vol. 4 (Box S206) Messerschmitt docket: Aktennotiz, Messerschmitt für Piel, Hentzen und Bringewald, 7 Jan 1941: 'Me-110 des H. Hess', Nachlass Messerschmitt.

FD4355/45 vol. 4 (Box S206) Unpublished Atkenvermerk Prof W. Messerschmitt an Herrn Caroli, Nr 92/41, v. 2 May 1941.


*National Air and Space Museum*, Smithsonian Institution, Archives Division, Washington DC

Reel 2963, F 199 *Untersuchungen über die Flatterneigung des Sporns, Me110D* (Test for tail wheel shimmying), Aug 1940.

Reel 2497, F 698 *Versuchsflug Flatter Bremsen Bf110E W.Nr.3850 NM+IX* (Test flight to observe effect of 'flutter brakes'), May 1941.

Reel 8168, I.P. No. 2746 *Bf110 mit 2 motoren DB601A oder DB601N (KBA-FI)*.


*National Archives and Records Administration*, Washington DC

T-177, Roll 19, RLM 226 *C-Amts-Monatsmeldung* (Technical Department Monthly Report) *für April 1941, Programm 19.2 vom 15.3.41*.

T-177, Roll 19, RLM 226 *Richtigstellung d. Progr. 18* (Amendment to Programme), *Ausgabe 3 vom 1.11.40*, 7 Jan 1941.

T-177, Roll 19, RLM 233 *Soll-u.1st – Ablieferung der Flugzeuge* (Estimated and Actual Delivery of Aircraft), 19 April 1940.

T-177, Roll 19, RLM 233 *Umschaltung* (Change-over) *110C2/C4/C6/D0/D0/-B/E-1*, 22 Jun 1940.

T-177, Roll 19, RLM 233 *Lieferplan* (Delivery Plan) *Nr.17c*, 3 July 1940.

*Public Record Office*, Kew

AIR 16/235 Fighter Command Intelligence Summary, Jan–Dec 1941.

AIR 16/365 Order of Battle, Fighter Command, Jun 1940–Apl 1942.

AIR 16/519 Feb–May 1941. Hitler: Proposed abduction to England by his private pilot.

AIR 16/698 War Room Log, Mar–Jly 1941.

AIR 16/1266 Royal Observer Corps: Flight of Rudolf Hess.

AIR 19/564 Duke of Hamilton: allegations concerning Rudolf Hess, Jan–Jly 1941.

AIR 22/73 War Room Daily Summaries, Oct 1940–Feb 1941.

AIR 22/78 War Room Daily Summaries, Apl–Sep 1943.

AIR 22/116 Air Ministry and War Room Summary, May 1941.

AIR 25/233 13 Group Operations Record Book, Jun 1941–Dec 1943.

AIR 27/442 43 Squadron Operations Record Book, Jan–Dec 1941.

AIR 27/460 46 Squadron Operations Record Book, Apl 1916–Dec 1943.

AIR 27/624 72 Squadron Operations Record Book, Jly 1917–Dec 1942.

AIR 27/969 141 Squadron Operations Record Book, Oct 1939–Dec 1941.

AIR 27/1706 317 Squadron Operations Record Book, Feb–Dec 1941.

AIR 27/2075 602 Squadron Operations Record Book, Jan–Dec 1941.

AIR 27/2079 603 Squadron Operations Record Book, Sep 1925–Dec 1943.

AIR 28/40 Ayr Operations Record Book, Jan 1941–Sep 1944.

AIR 28/219 Drem Operations Record Book, Oct 1929–Apl 1945.

AIR 28/624 Ouston Operations Record Book, Mar 1941–Jly 1942.

AIR 28/861 Turnhouse Operations Record Book, Aug 1936–Dec 1940.

AIR 28/864 Turnhouse Operations Record Book, Appendices, Jan–Nov 1941.

AIR 29/1019 63 MU Operations Record Book, Sep 1939–Dec 1946.

AIR 40/195 Messerschmitt Aircraft, Apl 1939–Mar 1945.

AIR 41/17 Air Defence of Great Britain, vol. III: Night Fighter Air Defence.

CAB 118/56 Correspondence concerning Hess, 1941.

DEFE 1/134 Rudolf Hess: censorship of mail, 1941.

FO 115/3544 British Embassy, Washington files: flight of Hess, 1941.

FO 181/969/12 Moscow Embassy: Correspondence concerning Hess, 1942.

FO 371/26565 Flight of Rudolf Hess to Scotland, 1941.

FO 371/26566 Flight of Rudolf Hess to Scotland, 1941.

FO 371/30920 Parliamentary statement on Rudolf Hess, 1942.

FO 371/30941 Nazi explanation of the mission of Herr Hess, 1942.

FO 371/33036 Soviet criticisms of British policy towards Hess, 1942.

FO 371/34484 Rudolf Hess, 1943.

FO 371/50976 German War Criminals, 1945.

FO 371/50986 German War Criminals, 1945.

FO 371/50993 German War Criminals, 1945.

FO 371/51001 German War Criminals: minutes of Nuremberg trials, 1945.

FO 371/57564 War Crimes: Trial of Hess, 1946.

FO 371/93535 Germany general (C). Treatment of War Criminals, 1951.

FO 371/93544 Germany general (C). Treatment of War Criminals, 1951.

FO 371/97970 Germany general (C). Treatment of War Criminals, 1952.

FO 371/103732 Conditions of War Criminals in Spandau Prison, 1953.

FO 371/118429 Consideration of cases of German War Criminals while in prison, 1955.

FO 371/124690 War Criminals in Spandau Prison, 1956.

FO 371/124691 War Criminals in Spandau Prison, 1956.

FO 371/124692 War Criminals in Spandau Prison, 1956.

FO 371/130852 War Criminals in Spandau Prison, 1957.

FO 371/130853 War Criminals in Spandau Prison, 1957.

FO 371/146063 Publications of Federal German Republic, 1959.

FO 371/146064 Prisoners in Spandau Prison, West Berlin, 1959.

FO 371/154293 Incarceration of German War Criminals in Spandau Prison, 1960.

FO 1093/1 Conversations between Hess and various officials, May–Jun 1941.

FO 1093/2 Translations of personal correspondence, Aug–Dec 1941.

FO 1093/3 Translations of personal correspondence, Dec 1941–Dec 1942.

FO 1093/4 Translations of personal correspondence, Feb 1942–Dec 1943.

FO 1093/5 Correspondence between War Office and PoW Reception Station, Abergavenny, Jun 1941–Oct 1945.

FO 1093/6 Possible exploitation of Hess incident for propaganda purposes, 1942.

FO 1093/7 Memorandum by O'Neill on propaganda use of Hess, 1941.

FO 1093/8 General correspondence on Camp Z, 1941–1944.

FO 1093/9 Proposal to call Hess in libel action, 1941.

FO 1093/10 Conversations between Hess and various officials, 1941.

FO 1093/11 Conversations between Hess and various officials, 1940–41.

FO 1093/12 Conversations between Hess and various officials, 1941.

FO 1093/13 Conversations between Hess and various officials, 1941.

FO 1093/14 Correspondence between War Office and Camp Z, 1941.

FO 1093/15 Correspondence between War Office and Camp Z, 1942.

FO 1093/16 Correspondence with Swiss Legation, records of visits to Maindiff Court, translations of personal correspondence, 1942–1943.

FO 1093/17 Correspondence with Swiss Legation, records of visits to Maindiff Court, translations of personal correspondence, 1944.

FO 1093/18 Correspondence with Swiss Legation, records of visits to Maindiff Court, translations of personal correspondence, 1945.

FO 1093/19 Correspondence with Swiss Legation, records of visits to Maindiff Court, translations of personal correspondence, 1945.

FO 1093/20 Notes on personal correspondence, 1944.

HO 144/22492/863753 Rudolf Hess: public disquiet and rumours about his mission, 1941–1942.

HO 199/305 Auxiliary petrol tanks jettisoned from British and German aircraft, 1940–1945.

HO 199/482 Messages about Hess's landing in Scotland, 1941.

HO 201/9 Ministry of Home Security, Daily Reports May–Jun 1941.

HO 324/1 Register of Prison Burials 1834–1969.

HS 6/623 Operation Foxley: plan to liquidate Hitler and/or his satellites.

HS 6/624 Operation Foxley, undated.

HS 6/625 Operation Foxley, 1944–1945.

HS 6/626 Little Foxleys, 1945.

INF 1/912 Ministry of Information: Rudolf Hess, 1941–1945.

KV 2/34 MI5 Documents relating to Hess, 12 May 1941–20 May 1941.

KV 2/35 MI5 Documents relating to Hess, 20 May 1941–07 Jun 1941.

KV 2/36 MI5 Documents relating to Hess, 05 Jun 1941–30 Jun 1941.

KV 2/37 MI5 Documents relating to Hess, 30 Jun 1941–08 Apl 1945.

KV 2/38 MI5 Documents relating to Hess, 14 Apl 1945–28 Mar 1946.

PREM 3/219/1 Hess: Effect in USA, Jun 1941.

PREM 3/219/2 Hess: Medical Report, Aug 1941.

PREM 3/219/3 Duke of Hamilton's Libel Action, Jun–Jly 1941.

PREM 3/219/4 Hess: Public Statements, May 1941.

PREM 3/219/5 Hess: Interview with Dr Guthrie, Jun 1941.

PREM 3/219/6 Hess: Soviet attitude and report by Lord Privy Seal, Oct–Nov 1942.

PREM 3/219/7 Various, May 1941, Sep 1943, Apl–May 1955.

PREM 3/434/7 Records of Meetings and Conversations, Oct–Dec 1944.

TS 27/510 Question of whether Hess should be subpoenaed in Duke of Hamilton's libel suit, 1941.

WO 166/1260 War Diaries, Home Forces, Bedfordshire, Huntingdonshire, Northamptonshire, Jun 1940–Dec 1941.

WO 166/1293 War Diaries, Home Force, North East London HQ, Apl–Dec 1941.

WO 166/2293 Headquarters 49 AA Brigade, Sep 1939–Dec 1941.

WO 199/3288A Scottish Command – The Capture of Rudolf Hess.

WO 199/3288B Scottish Command – The Capture of Rudolf Hess.

WO 208/4471 MI14 dossier on Hess, 1941–55.

# Index